Creating Calm Classrooms

Creating Calm Classrooms

Teacher Behavior and Management Practices that Work

Andrew T. Kulemeka

ROWMAN & LITTLEFIELD
Lanham • Boulder • New York • London

Published by Rowman & Littlefield
An imprint of The Rowman & Littlefield Publishing Group, Inc.
4501 Forbes Boulevard, Suite 200, Lanham, Maryland 20706
www.rowman.com

6 Tinworth Street, London SE11 5AL

British Library Cataloguing in Publication Information Available

Library of Congress Cataloging-in-Publication Data Is Available

ISBN 978-1-4758-5064-2 (cloth: alk. paper)
ISBN 978-1-4758-5065-9 (pbk: alk. paper)
ISBN 978-1-4758-5066-6 (electronic)

∞ ™ The paper used in this publication meets the minimum requirements of American National Standard for Information Sciences Permanence of Paper for Printed Library Materials, ANSI/NISO Z39.48-1992.

I dedicate this book to all teachers in the United States who work tirelessly, selflessly, and with unrequited dedication to educate millions of children. Their work is very ordinary and unglamorous and does not receive any Oscars. They bear the brunt of middle and high school adolescent moods, insolence, and self-centeredness with equanimity and patience. These teachers are the foundation stones upon which is built this most developed and powerful country in the world.

Contents

Preface

There Are No Bad Students, Just Poorly Managed Classrooms

OBJECTIVE

Teachers will learn that they have the means to create the classes they desire.

A common refrain from frustrated teachers that I have heard in the twenty years that I have spent teaching in public secondary schools is, "I have a bad group of students." As a mentor teacher, when I visited some of those teachers' classes, the evidence of total chaos was abundant. In one instance, several students were out of their seats walking around the classroom despite the teacher's shrill shouts that they sit down.

Other students had their heads on desks soundly sleeping. On most desks, in large permanent markers, students had boldly scribbled curse words, and some students were actively engaged in animated conversations that had nothing to do with the lesson the teacher was attempting to teach; in fact, some students had turned their backs to the chalkboard.

Still, six or seven students were standing at the door, unwilling to follow the teacher's loud and repeated instructions to get inside and take their seats. The whole class was completely out of control, and the teacher was totally ineffective. When I looked at the teacher, he helplessly shrugged his shoulders and looked at me with a look that seemed to say, "I told you these are bad kids." It seemed impossible not to agree with him that these were indeed bad students. However, after sitting down, I noticed several students whom I had seen behave so well in other classes acting in totally unacceptable ways in this teacher's class. There were even three or four who were so well-behaved in my class but were exhibiting such outrageous behavior for this teacher that I was inevitably confronted with the question: Why this radical difference in behavior in the same students?

After visiting this teacher for three weeks, I noticed that his lesson for those three full weeks consisted of a student doing a short timed sprint in front of the class. It was a three-minute demonstration about speed and distance. This teacher expected his students to focus their attention on this three-minute demonstration for many one-and-a-half hour lessons for three weeks. Clearly, he had nothing to teach but somehow expected his students to just sit quietly as nothing happened in his class.

The following year, I mentored a teacher who was assigned an honors class. I witnessed the sad, precipitous descent of an honors class into a rowdy inferno of loud, defiant, and unruly students. My observation of the class also revealed that the teacher did not have any plans for what she was going to teach daily; she compensated for the lack of lesson plans with her incessant chatter and sarcasm. She seemed to hope that ridiculing students would intimidate them and earn her a quiet environment.

On the contrary, the class became an unmanageable, relentless zoo of chattering, desk-banging rude students; some students amused themselves by throwing textbooks through the window. After these two experiences, I noticed that, whenever there were serious classroom management problems with a class as a whole, the teacher and not the students was the cause. Almost invariably, there appeared to be a lack of worthwhile teaching in the classes.

In other words, there were really no bad students; there were just incompetent teachers. This is not to deny that a very tiny minority of students want to undermine a teacher's efforts to teach and create conditions that can prevent instruction from occurring; fortunately for us, such students are few: two or three in the hard classes and none in most classes. My point here is that such a minority can be managed to a point where it is ineffectual and ceases to adversely affect instruction.

Through a combination of strategies encompassing careful planning for instruction, consistency in high academic expectations, frequent monitoring of student learning and behavior, use of technology to facilitate communication with parents and guardians, and the establishment of routines and procedures that make classes predictable, any teacher can eliminate the misbehavior of the few and manage classes in which instruction proceeds smoothly.

The goal of this book is to make explicit patterns of teacher behaviors and management practices that I have observed effective teachers use and have also found effective in managing my own classrooms. Thus, this book is different from the majority of other books on classroom management because it stems primarily from my work as a teacher and mentor teacher. My experiences with middle and high school students have shown me that certain deliberate actions by a teacher can create environments in which learning can smoothly occur.

The motivation for writing this book is to make coherent and systematic what I practiced and have observed in effective teachers. It is this body of knowledge that has assisted new and experienced struggling teachers that I present in this book. This book does not reduce the complex process of managing classrooms to a bag of tricks that a teacher just needs to be aware of, as a good number of books seem to indicate.

In the bag of tricks tradition, a student's misbehavior is countered with a certain act by the teacher that supposedly "neutralizes" the misconduct. Rather, my approach in this book is to forestall off-task behaviors before they occur. To achieve such a goal presupposes the knowledge that effective classroom management stems from the intersection of the nuts and bolts of creating routines, procedures, and other "furniture" aspects of the class, on the one hand, and sustaining a classroom environment of high academic expectations, on the other.

From the confluence of the furniture of managing a class well and maintaining an academic class climate that is consistently challenging arises effectively run classrooms in which students' misbehaviors are totally minimized and often completely eliminated.

In truly well-run classrooms, students' misconduct is not given a chance to be expressed because the important business of learning is always given priority by both the teacher and the students. Thus, well-managed classes are also classes with the highest academic achievements for students.

Even though failure to successfully manage classrooms accounts for the majority of the reasons new teachers leave teaching, many studies indicate that preservice instruction on classroom management in most teacher training institutions is seriously inadequate (Jones, 2006[1]; Stough, 2006[2]). Among the numerous weaknesses in preservice teacher training, Jones reports that there is often a lack of understanding among most professors of education because they do not have recent or any practical experience with managing classrooms themselves; therefore, the scant attention that some of them pay to classroom management tends to be impractical.

This book arises from practical experiences with my own classes and my mentoring of new and struggling experienced teachers. Following the advice presented here should help any teacher realize a class climate most suitable for teaching and learning; in turn, students achieve high levels of learning as a result.

Yet, still, some of the available books on managing students' behaviors approach the topic through scenarios. Often, such scenarios present an acute situation of student misbehavior, and then, the professor offers some possible ways of handling the situation. While the situations and solutions seem plausible enough, they do not really prepare student teachers for the complex situations that arise in classrooms. Rarely do difficulties with managing student behaviors begin with extreme moments of misconduct, defiance, or insubordination.

Frequently, a teacher's challenges to classroom management start, not with extreme and clear outburst of misconduct, but with little and seemingly inconsequential incidents: a whisper to another student when the teacher is talking or an innocent smile to the teacher while a student is passing a piece of paper to another during instruction.

Anticipating and preempting such occurrences becomes critical to how a teacher fares with his or her class over the course of a year. In other words, this book is different from most of the books on managing student behaviors because it systematically provides the reader with procedures, routines, sets of deliberate actions, and a system of behaviors that would unfailingly preempt the challenging student behaviors that other authors of books on classroom management take as givens and attempt to provide methods of handling.

There are no scenarios in this book about what you should do when a student, for example, uses profanity. Employing the methods suggested in this book creates a classroom climate in which students do not attempt to use profanity or other language that demeans others or disrupts the learning atmosphere.

I recall hearing a mentor teacher I had during my first year of teaching in a middle school say, "You can create the class that you desire. It is all up to you." At the time, I did not believe her as I daily struggled with the forty-seven eighth-graders I had accepted to teach in January because a popular teacher had unexpectedly quit. Under normal circumstances, with a class of twenty-five to thirty students, it is indeed true that the class that a teacher desires is the one she or he ends up with.

If the class is unruly, it is the teacher who has created such a class; similarly, if the class is well behaved, it is the teacher who should get credit for it. It follows then that it is really false to speak of good or bad students because how students behave is entirely a reflection of the teacher's expectations of that class.

Some writers on classroom management present a false dichotomy between the skills of managing a classroom and teaching. Under skills for managing a classroom, for example, fall such acts as the creation of predictable patterns of conduct that become so internalized that students accept and use them without creating undue stress on the teacher.

Consequently, students' behavior becomes so automated that there is little need on the part of the teacher to constantly teach students how to act in certain routine situations, such as shelving books, dismissal at the end of class, submitting homework and classwork, finding missed work when a student has been absent, responding to questions in class, seeking permission to leave class, and many other situations that occur regularly in classrooms.

While, in fact, routines and procedures significantly contribute to better classroom management, by themselves, they cannot sustain optimal conditions for learning. Effective teachers know that getting students to promptly settle down and stop talking in one's classroom, for instance, is just the beginning. Such good behavior might last for three to five minutes before chaos descends on the class again. What preempts such chaos is the timely insertion of meaningful learning; without learning that students understand as important and relevant, the behaviorist-driven routines and procedures simply fail.

However, by the same token, while good lesson plans and knowledgeable teachers do gain a measure of respect from their students on the basis of their superior knowledge, impressive command of knowledge by itself does not lead to good classroom management. As stated already, effective classroom management occurs at the confluence of an awareness of the routines and procedures of managing a class (the furniture of classroom management), on the one hand, and the adeptness by the teacher in sustaining a class climate of meaningful and adequately challenging instruction, on the other. It is these twin streams and how they constantly intersect in the classroom that is the business of this book.

An effective teacher's skillful manipulation of both streams accounts for his or her success in managing classes. Reading this book will enable teachers, regardless of their years of teaching experience, to effectively manage their classrooms and preempt the off-task behaviors that derail good lesson plans.

NOTES

1. Jones, V. (2006). How do teachers learn to be effective classroom managers? In C. M. Evertson & C. S. Weinstein (Eds.), *Handbook of classroom management: Research, practice, and contemporary issues* (pp. 887–907). Mahwah, NJ: Lawrence Erlbaum Publishers.

2. Stough, L. M. (2006). The place of classroom management and standards in teacher education. In C. M. Evertson & C. S. Weinstein (Eds.), *Handbook of classroom management: Research, practice, and contemporary issues* (pp. 909–923). Mahwah, NJ: Lawrence Erlbaum Publishers.

Acknowledgments

The genesis of this book can be traced back to January 1999 when I was offered an English position at Kettering Middle School, Prince George's County Public Schools, to teach forty-seven eighth-grade students. As soon as I began teaching that class, it was clear to me that I was lacking in fundamental classroom management knowledge. Even though I had successfully taught university students in the United States and Malawi, I simply had no idea how to manage an American suburban middle school class. I am grateful to my mentor teacher and particularly to my department chair who offered to teach some classes for me to observe.

I also thank Prof. Bob Ramsey, University of Maryland, College Park, then chair of Asian and East European languages for providing me the position of research associate with the University of Maryland, which enabled me to borrow books from the library and do extensive research on classroom management. Without his assistance, it would have been hard to have access to the vast resources that the University of Maryland, College Park, main library holds.

I have also benefited from the position of being a mentor teacher at Bowie High School, which allowed me to witness firsthand the difficulties that new teachers and struggling experienced teachers faced with respect to managing classes. It was as I attempted to explain to such teachers what needed to be done that I realized that there was vast knowledge that I needed to share in a systematic way to help them manage their classes.

I also learned a great deal from my interactions with colleagues at Bowie High School, principally through "learning walks." As we systematically visited each other's classes, we learned from each other what worked well and what did not. I was privileged to visit both very effective and noneffective teachers. I reflected on those experiences and compared them with my own way of running my classes.

During my tenure at Bowie High School, I grew immensely from regularly teaching at least one cotaught class each year, which had a significant number of special education students. Students with ADD or ADHD and other learning disorders may present special classroom management challenges. I am grateful to have had such classes because they sharpened my classroom management skills to the extent that students' behaviors in those classes were as good as or even better than in regular or honors classes.

I recall a compliment that Mr. Rapple, a retired Bowie High School social studies teacher, made after visiting my cotaught class: "Dr. K (my nickname at Bowie), you should be a consultant on classroom management when you retire." Mr. Rapple could not believe that the class he was observing was a cotaught class with a lot of special education students. The students were impeccably well behaved.

Lastly, I would like to acknowledge the support my family has given me over the years that I have taught in Prince George's County Public School. I thank my wife, Mel, and daughters, Moyenda and Chikondi, for listening to my endless stories of joys and frustrations as I worked in the school system. I am particularly thankful to my family for their support during the sudden loss of our son. Their love and support made it possible for me to continue working even when it felt like there was no meaning to life.

Introduction

The material in this book is organized in the following fashion. Chapter 1 discusses what every teacher needs to do before the first day of school. A serious level of preparation needs to be made before students appear in the classroom on your first day. Such preparation can lead to one having a successful year; failure to prepare leads to a disastrous beginning, which can be very hard to recover from. As I point out in chapter 1, there is a small window of opportunity that teachers have during the first two weeks at the beginning of the school year that, if utilized well, establishes well-managed classes for the rest of the school year.

Chapter 2 dwells on the importance of lesson preparation and pacing to successful lessons. Effective teachers are prepared every day to teach and have a clear sense of how their lessons will proceed. A teacher's lack of preparation is very quickly noticed by students and severely undermines one's authority in the classroom. In cases where the teacher demonstrates lack of preparation frequently, students may take advantage of the uncertainty in the teacher to create a climate of disrespect and disruption.

Related to preparation is pacing. When a teacher is prepared, he or she knows how long to dwell on one topic before moving on to the next and what would mark a good transition from one topic to the next. Such assuredness on the part of the teacher cultivates a sense of trust in the students and enables the teacher to have the support of the majority of the students. In turn, such support minimizes or entirely eliminates discipline problems for the teacher.

Chapter 3 discusses the role that communication with students and parents plays in managing students' behaviors in classrooms. The chapter shows that teachers have to find less burdensome and more efficient ways of communicating with parents and students regularly. Failure to communicate with parents promptly exacerbates problems that a teacher may have experienced in a class. As a result, he or she does not benefit from the important support that most parents provide to teachers when their assistance is sought in a timely manner.

From the first day of school to the last, teachers should always be ready to contact parents whenever a student acts in ways that makes the smooth running of the class challenging. When students know that their teacher does not hesitate to contact parents, they are always mindful of how they behave in his or her class.

Chapter 4 demonstrates with clear examples the idea of sustaining a classroom environment of high expectations. In this chapter, it is shown that one can not only create a climate of high expectations but also sustain it. In a goal-driven classroom where the teacher is very clear about what he or she wants his or her students to achieve, there is an inherent sense of urgency. The goals provide a strong impetus to the lessons, and such energy is communicated to the students and parents as lessons unfold. At every point in the course of the school year, the teacher is constantly aware about where he or she wants the students to be at the end of the school year or semester.

Chapter 5 presents methods for managing students' misbehavior. While the preceding chapters provide a framework for preempting students' misbehavior, chapter 5 acknowledges that there may be instances, rare in well-managed classes, when some form of misbehavior may develop. The techniques suggested in this chapter can minimize and eliminate such misbehaviors.

At the heart of the strategies suggested in chapter 5 is the idea of constantly monitoring the classroom. Teachers who are continuously aware of whatever is happening in their classrooms have an excellent chance of stopping misbehavior before it mushrooms into serious class disruption. Teachers who are occupied with their e-mail messages, texts, and other distractions are likely to pay for such lack of constant monitoring of their classes through unfortunate acts of serious disruptions to their classrooms.

Chapter 6 examines the idea of teacher expectations. Teaching, unlike the majority of other professions, sets a very high bar for the expectations it has for its teachers. Since teachers are role models, there are a number of areas of teacher conduct that teachers need to be aware of. For example, schools tend to emphasize the importance of students' being punctual to class. For such an expectation to be effectively implemented in a school, it follows that teachers themselves have to set an example, for to insist that students arrive on time while teachers are routinely late is hypocritical and often fails in grade schools.

This book gives practical advice to new and experienced teachers who would like to manage their classrooms well. My views on classroom management have developed primarily from my own reflections on this topic and my exposure to poorly run classes as I worked as a mentor teacher helping new and struggling experienced teachers. I have also augmented my experiences with extensive reading on classroom management.

It is through my observation and efforts to assist other teachers that the idea of writing this book came about. As I attempted to explain the essentials of classroom management to teachers who were overwhelmed and frustrated with the chaotic classes they had to face daily, I realized that there was so much that I needed to tell them; it was practically impossible to tell them everything without creating a sense that there was just too much to learn. For instance, I realized that there was a lot that the struggling or new teacher needed to have done before the first day of school to avoid the problems that he or she was experiencing in the sixth week of the school year.

As a mentor teacher, I was usually approached by my principal or an assistant principal to assist a struggling teacher two or three months after the school year had begun. Unfortunately, I often felt that the teacher was already in such deep trouble that what I wanted to do to help him or her had a limited chance of succeeding. Good classroom management starts weeks before the school year has begun and needs to be sustained every day in every lesson. The critical period when a teacher's classroom management fundamentals have to be laid down during the first two weeks of the beginning of the school year has to be maximally utilized for a smooth year for the teacher.

Any teacher who follows the suggestions made in this book should have well-managed classes in which students' misbehavior has no chance of developing into a problem. He or she should have the kind of peaceful classes that I enjoyed every year when I taught in public schools in Maryland in the United States.

KEY IDEAS IN THIS SECTION

- When a class becomes impossible to manage, the fault is not with the students; it is with the teacher. Most classes will have one or two so-called difficult students who may be quite willing to disrupt good lessons; the majority of students, 98 percent or more, are ready and keen to learn.
- Knowledge of good classroom management skills and a commitment to teaching should guarantee an environment in which students learn and a teacher teaches successfully.
- The knowledge discussed in this book will transform any novice or anxious teacher into one who knows how to manage his or her class smoothly.

REFLECTION QUESTIONS

1. What kind of classes do you want to have this year and how will you ensure that happens?
2. What connections do you see between managing a class well and students' academic growth?
3. Why should managing a class well be every teacher's primary concern?

Chapter One

What Happens before School Starts and the Critical First Weeks of School?

OBJECTIVES

1. Teachers will learn about what preparations have to be made before students arrive.
2. Teachers will learn what information needs to be presented to students on the first day of school.
3. Teachers will learn strategies for ensuring that students learn routines and procedures that support classroom management.

Even after many years of teaching in secondary schools in the United States, I am still surprised by how well all students behave during the first few weeks of the school year. Some authors of classroom management explain this phenomenon in terms of the fact that students do not know each other and are therefore intimidated by the new environment; others state that students are ready to learn having found summer too long and boring. Whatever accounts for this phenomenon, the fact is that the teacher has a small critical window of opportunity to begin to put in place what kind of class he or she will have for the rest of the year.

Due to the fact that such a window is indeed very brief, teachers need to plan for it several weeks before the first day of school; in fact, an effective teacher knows that he or she has to be fully ready when the students arrive on the first day of school. There is just no room for mistakes beginning on that first day of school.

FURNITURE ARRANGEMENT IN THE CLASSROOM: STUDENTS' DESKS

Before the first day of school, teachers should make sure that they have received class rosters, which inform them about how many students they are to expect in their classes. This is vital information because it determines the number of desks a teacher should have in his or her class. To be safe, one always prepares for more students than one may actually receive; therefore, if the class roster shows that you will receive twenty-five students, it is better to get thirty desks. It is better to have more desks than to have a student standing in your classroom because there is no seat for him or her.

The next important step here is to arrange the desks in such a way that the teacher is able to easily reach the desk of every student in the class. The teacher's circulation in the class should not be hampered by furniture or any other obstacles. Easily reaching students serves two important purposes. First, a teacher should be able to reach the desk of any student in the class and assist whomever needs help; failure to do so because of poor arrangement of furniture should be viewed as a very serious handicap to teaching. Second, reaching all students allows the teacher to manage his or her class well.

When students are inattentive or distracted in some way, the teacher should be able to come next to the desk of the concerned students to remind them of what is happening in the class; this has to be done unobtrusively and promptly. Therefore, as desks are being arranged in the classroom, the teacher should make sure that he or she will be able to easily reach each student in the classroom without tripping over backpacks or shoes or being blocked by students' desks and other furniture.

Teachers who wear shoes that do not create noise have some advantages over those who wear shoes that are loud as they move in the classroom. One advantage of noiseless shoes is that the teacher can move unnoticeably within the class and sometimes surprise a student who is not paying attention by being right next to him or her, unannounced so to speak. These kinds of surprises are useful for purposes of ensuring that all students are on task. During tests and quizzes, silent shoes enable a teacher to walk behind the backs of the students, monitoring the exams without the students always being aware of the exact position where the teacher is standing.

THE TEACHER'S DESK AND OTHER ITEMS OF COMMON USE

Once students' desks are arranged, the teacher's desk and other furniture need to be situated. The teacher has to consider where and why some furniture and items of regular use are placed. A desk that will be used for receiving students' assignments has to be easily accessible to all students in the class. Items such as a class pencil sharpener, stapler, dictionaries, and class sets of textbooks should be placed where students can easily reach them without bumping into each other; alternatively, the teacher needs to think of a system for how students would reach such items without creating traffic jams within the class.

Similarly, the teacher's desk and chest of drawers need to be located in places with less student traffic. In particular, the teacher's desk should be away from zones where students tend to congregate or to travel a lot for reasons of privacy. Often, teachers receive confidential memoranda, such as students' requests for letters of reference, individual education programs (IEPs), 504 plans, and other correspondence. It is clearly unprofessional and inappropriate for students to be able to read such materials on the teacher's desk before they are filed.

Owing to the fact that a teacher may sometimes be so busy during the school year that he or she may not immediately file such correspondence and might therefore leave it lying around on his or her desk for several days, it is extremely important that the teacher's desk be located in a place that students cannot easily reach; there should be a zone of privacy in that area.

In addition, cables to printers, computers, and LCD projectors should be away from zones of heavy student traffic where they do not pose a problem to either students or the equipment to which they are attached.

Effective teachers visualize the movements of their students and themselves as they decide where to place various items in their classes.

SEATING CHARTS AND THEIR IMPORTANCE

Other important items that need to be ready before the first day of school are class seating charts. These kinds of seating charts are primarily designed using the alphabetical arrangements of the names on the class rosters. Nonetheless, placing students in seats before the first day of school fulfills many important functions. An obvious, but nonetheless important, role of a seating chart is that it enables you to know who you have in your class. For example, there may be two Amanda Smiths in your class or three Taylors. How will you distinguish them? If you have already discovered this reality through the class roster as you were creating a seating chart, you may be better prepared for it.

A more important role of creating a seating chart is that it allows you to begin the critical task of learning your students' names. Beginning on that first day of school as you call students' names and tell them where to sit, you start the process of learning their names. Learning students' names quickly allows the teacher to personalize immediately his or her interactions with the class; students feel a sense of belonging and care from a teacher who prompt-ly identifies them by their names.

The opposite situation, in which a teacher has no seating chart and for weeks continues to show his or her ignorance of students' names, conveys to the students a lack of care for who they are. Unwittingly, students get the impression that they do not matter enough for this teacher to take the time to learn who they are; let us not forget that your students know your name on the first day of the school year.

Creating seating charts, which enable teachers to quickly learn students' names, also becomes useful if a teacher needs to contact a parent for some-thing about a student. A seating chart identifies the student by name, and therefore, the teacher can call a parent using such information if there is need. Some minor or potentially major problems can be taken care of during the first days of the school year using seating charts.

And yet another reason why a seating chart created out of a class roster is still very useful is because it allows a teacher to separate students who are friends and who might want to sit next to each other. If students are allowed to sit where they want, they will normally want to sit next to their friends, and such sitting arrangements can be a source of excessive talking and class disruption.

In addition, a seating chart that a teacher uses from the moment students walk into his or her class establishes unequivocally who decides in the class where students sit. It seems a trivial point, but you can imagine a classroom in which the teacher does not decide where students sit turning into a class where some students change seats daily because they feel like doing so.

Furthermore, you can also envision a situation arising in a classroom where a student refuses to be moved to a seat because he or she has been allowed to sit wherever he or she has wanted in the past. This could become a whole class problem where the teacher has lost authority and students as a whole class refuse to be assigned seats because they were allowed to sit wherever they wanted at the beginning of the school year.

Assigning students seats establishes the teacher's authority in the class from the moment students enter his or her classroom, and this simple practice gives a teacher the freedom to change students' seats whenever he or she notices that some students are socializing too much in the classroom and therefore need to be separated.

As the year goes by and teachers get to know their students' behaviors better, seating arrangements may be altered to reflect such knowledge. But no teacher should begin the school year without a seating chart already in place on the first day of school.

CLASSROOM DECORATIONS

Classroom decorations are another area of class preparation that has an impact on students' perceptions about a teacher and the class. Clearly, a classroom that is not well decorated conveys a sense of lack of interest from the teacher; unfortunately, classroom decorations are just like the clothes the teacher wears. Just as people make judgments about others on the basis of the clothes they wear, students too make deductions about a class on the strength of whether the teacher has made the effort to change it into an attractive learning environment.

A sense of serious concern for students' learning is also communicated by the evidence of care that the teacher has revealed in transforming old, spotted, ugly white walls into a beautiful classroom. The attractive learning climate speaks directly to the students, announcing this teacher means business in this class. By the same token, a classroom with bare walls or some ugly posters screams to the students that they should not expect very much from this teacher who has not bothered to get his or her room ready.

We have all been to classrooms where the desks were scattered around haphazardly and the walls bare or with a few token decorations, some of which had nothing to do with the class. In one math class, for example, there was one large poster of an ugly looking calculator. Looking around the classroom, one keenly felt the sense that the teacher was somehow careless and unconcerned about students' learning. In fact, the classroom itself communicated a feeling of endless boredom, a long gray year to be endured by students; no parent could trust that teacher to teach his or her child.

In contrast, we have also been to classrooms that were bright and welcoming. The wall decorations and bulletin boards were full of inviting, thought-provoking posters. Sitting in such classrooms, one had a good feeling about the teachers of such classes, even though one had not seen them teach. We cannot minimize the impact that our classroom decorations have on students. While posters do not teach or sustain an environment of academic high expectations, they certainly contribute to creating the feeling of a good classroom when we use them well.

THE FIRST DAY OF SCHOOL

The first day of school stands out as one of the most important days of the school year. Wong and Wong[1] go so far as to claim that everything that happens in the rest of the school year is determined by how teachers handle the first day. The first day of school allows a teacher to set the right tone for his or her class. Thus, using the seating charts to assign students' seats, which are arranged in a manner that facilitates the teacher's circulation among students, the teacher clearly communicates his or her expectations in these actions that have preceded the arrival of students.

The level of preparedness is a powerful message to students that, in this classroom, their time will be treated as the precious commodity that it is.

CLASSROOM RULES

Classroom rules are one of the first things that a teacher needs to address on the first day of school. Good classroom rules need to be all encompassing and limited in number. For example, the following three class rules may suffice for middle and high schools:

1. Respect yourself, others, and property.
2. Come to class prepared to learn.
3. Do not eat, drink, or chew gum in class.

In order for students to feel that they have ownership in the formulation of the rules, it is always a good idea to allow them to discuss the rules. The teacher may begin the discussion by asking the class, for instance, why it is a good idea to "respect oneself"?

At the beginning of the school year, a discussion of this sort may break the ice and allow students to begin to feel comfortable in the class. Without belaboring the issue, a teacher may conclude the discussion by summing up what the consensus opinion has been on each of the rules. He or she may also explain to the class how an absence of such rules would affect the class. It may also be a particularly relevant point to show students how some of the class rules are also school- or district-wide rules.

For example, most school districts have rules forbidding students from damaging school property. In the first rule, "respect property," a teacher may show the connection between such a class rule to the rule that forbids students from vandalizing or damaging school property, such as books, walls, desks, computers, and other things of that sort.

Similarly, the teacher may also show that the rule about "respect others" also expresses a school- or district-wide rule that forbids students from bullying each other. A teacher may explain that ill-treating other students verbally or physically, which is what bullying is, is not allowed in the classroom as well as the district or the school. It is important to show students that some of the class rules are in concert with district- or school-wide rules. Such connections give students a strong rationale for why the class rules are relevant.

The same argument about a rule being applied to the whole district or school can be said about the third rule above: "Do not eat, drink, or chew gum in class."

Most school districts do not want students to bring food to classrooms for primarily two reasons. First, grade school students tend to be clumsy with food and drinks and often end up spilling such things on the floor. Unfortunately, not all students who spill drinks or food are enthusiastic about cleaning up their mess, and even when they clean up, they tend not to be thorough. To avoid trash and dirty floors because of spilled sodas and fruit drinks, most schools and districts prohibit students from bringing food and drinks to classrooms.

The second reason for not allowing food and drinks in classrooms has to do with not wanting cockroaches, mice, or rats to flourish in classrooms. Such vermin bring diseases, and their presence in a classroom is very much discouraged. Thus, a lot of school districts and schools prohibit students from bringing food and drinks into classrooms.

These early discussions of the importance of class rules give a teacher a chance to begin to know his or her students. It is also at this point that a teacher starts to show his or her students how the class will be run. For example, if there is a student who tends to talk out of turn or interrupts others or the teacher, the teacher would have to start correcting such behavior in gentle and nonthreatening ways. If a student interrupts him or her, for example, the teacher may just stop talking and take a long pause while looking at the student who has interrupted him or her.

Sometimes, such actions may correct the behavior. If they do not, then the teacher may have to explicitly say that interrupting others is not welcome and whoever wants to share his or her opinion should raise a hand. If this explicit explanation still does not bring about the intended result with regard to one student who seems determined to not follow directions, a teacher may, even on this first day, write down the student's name, using the seating chart. He or she may decide to have a conversation with the student at the end of class.

If the student appears to deliberately disregard the teacher's expectations, he or she may call a parent on that first day of school to explain what the child has been doing.

It is never too early to ask for a parent's support; in fact, calling on the first day conveys to the parents and the noncompliant student that whoever chooses not to follow directions in this class should expect a consequence. Calling on the first day also sends a powerful message to the whole class that the current teacher will do whatever it takes to gain the cooperation of students in his or her class.

ROUTINES AND PROCEDURES

After the class rules, a teacher may explain some of the important routines and procedures. For example, when is a student late and what happens when the late arrival is excused or unexcused? How does a student obtain a pass to the bathroom or health room? How are movements within the class handled? For example, when is the appropriate time for a student to get up and get a tissue or sharpen a pencil? What happens when there are quizzes and tests?

The last point about quizzes and tests should be in the syllabus, and therefore, it may be appropriate at this point to hand out the syllabus. Students need to get copies of the syllabus on the first day of school. The syllabus is a serious document specifying terms of agreement between a teacher and his or her students regarding what the educational goals are for the class and the rules and policies that will guide the class toward achieving those goals; handing out the syllabus on the first day of school communicates to students that indeed school has started.

Once the syllabus has been explained and routines and procedures covered, a teacher may move very promptly to hand out textbooks. As soon as students have signed for their textbooks, the teacher may introduce the first lesson. It is a good idea to give students some homework on the first day of school. This is not just a gimmick; it is the beginning of school, and students learn quickly that the important work of studying has begun in earnest.

LEARNING THE CLASSROOM PROCEDURES AND ROUTINES

It is probably not an exaggeration that what ultimately distinguishes an experienced teacher who manages his or her classes well from someone who is either new to the profession or does not run classes well is the degree to which the veteran teacher demonstrates patience. To be an effective teacher, one invariably has to accept fully that learning occurs at varying paces for students. It does not matter what the material being taught is. Therefore, the class routines that a teacher explains on the first day of school and that are also included on the syllabus that students take home and share with their parents take time to be learned and accepted.

The teacher's responsibility is to teach the routines and make sure that all in the class know how to act accordingly. This is where a great deal of patience is required. Some students will need several weeks to learn and accept the routines. For example, if the teacher wants his or her students to raise their hands before they can answer or ask a question, he or she will have to teach the students this procedure. It is not enough to explain it on the first day and then expect all students to behave accordingly. The teacher should be ready and willing to spend several weeks reinforcing this practice in his or her students.

If the routine or procedure is important for the functioning of the class, then it is worth the teacher's time to teach it with patience and kindness. If, for example, there is a student who seems to persist in just getting out of his seat without the teacher's permission, the teacher should calmly remind him or her to ask for permission before getting out of his or her seat. This may go on for three or four weeks. The patience that the teacher shows in teaching the procedure is necessary and will ensure that the majority of the students will learn, without fear of being ridiculed, all the other procedures that the teacher considers important to the smooth running of his or her class.

Handled differently, the learning of classroom routines could turn out to be a source of conflict and irritation between the teacher and the students. Imagine a teacher who displays obvious frustration with his or her students because they do not seek permission before they get out of their seats. While the quick learners may have learned the routine on the first day, others might feel threatened and angry that the teacher is not giving them enough time and practice to learn the routine. His or her sign of frustration with them would create feelings of resentment and hostility.

If the teacher were insensitive enough to start deriding students who were not following the procedure, he or she could turn the whole process of learning classroom routines into a source of class disruption.

In short, shelving books, picking up trash on the floor at the end of a period, appropriate times to sharpen pencils, how to turn in notebooks and assignments, and any other routines that the teacher considers important need to be specifically taught to the class with patience for students to use them correctly.

TEACHING STUDENTS TO TAKE QUIZZES AND TESTS

Students need to be taught that, during quizzes and tests, they need to be absolutely quiet and not share information. While being quiet may seem obvious to adults, most students need some training and reminding about this. Again, it is not sufficient to put the rule of being quiet during tests on the syllabus; explain it on the first day of school, and get parents to read it in the syllabus and sign that they have read it.

Teachers who successfully conduct their quizzes and tests in classrooms where students do not talk and disrupt testing find it necessary to teach their students about how to conduct themselves during tests. This learning and internalization of the practice of taking quizzes and tests in silence may involve reminding students *every* time they are about to take a quiz or test Yes, you have read the sentence correctly; students need to be reminded every time they take a test, from the beginning of the school year to the end in June.

It also means mentioning the consequences of receiving a zero on the quiz or test if this rule is violated; the redundancy and repetition is necessary to ensure that no student forgets or pretends not to know the expectations. A teacher would also need to mention that cell phones or electronic devices are forbidden during quizzes and tests.

Most school districts penalize students with a zero if it is established that a student has cheated on a quiz or test by either talking or using an electronic device. A zero on a quiz or a test with many points can have a big adverse impact on a student's grade. Thus, it is important that a teacher makes certain that, when he or she assigns a zero, there is no doubt that the student violated the quiz and test requirement intentionally. To rule out forgetfulness or just lack of knowledge of the concerned rule, a teacher needs to repeat the expectations for quiz and test taking at the beginning of each quiz and test all the time.

Why repeat the expectation the whole year when it should be obvious to all students what they are supposed to do during quizzes and tests? The most important reason for repeating it has to do with ensuring that no student violates the regulation and suffers the consequence of receiving a zero on a quiz or test. Before a teacher can record a zero for a student who talked or disrupted or cheated on a test, it has to be abundantly clear to everyone in the classroom what the regulation is, and there should be no possibility of a student saying that he or she forgot or did not know. A zero on a quiz or test has an inordinate impact on a student's grade, and the student who receives such a grade should be absolutely clear why such a grade was deserved.

Second, most parents are concerned when a zero is recorded for an assessment task, such as a quiz or test. If a parent questions how his or her child received a zero on a test, the teacher should be able to explain that, at the beginning of the quiz or test, the class was reminded of the regulation regarding how quizzes and tests are conducted. It should be clear to all concerned that the child willfully violated the regulation. Note that it would not be sufficient if the teacher explained such a zero by merely referring to the fact that it was mentioned at the beginning of the school year and that it is also included on the syllabus.

Such an explanation would not suffice for the simple reason that a child might legitimately claim to have forgotten. Therefore, in order to preempt forgetfulness or other possible excuses, the teacher would do well to mention it at the beginning of every test; if it sounds repetitive, the better for students to learn it and not violate it.

WHAT TO DO ABOUT STUDENTS' CELL PHONES AND OTHER ELECTRONIC DEVICES DURING TESTS

Now that most school systems have accepted that students can bring their cell phones into classrooms, teachers have been confronted with a serious challenge regarding ensuring that the tests and quizzes that they administer are not compromised by students who take pictures of the tests and send them to their friends or search for answers to test questions on their cell phones. If not handled properly, a teacher risks being frustrated and overwhelmed with conflicts with students arising from the use of electronic devices during tests and when instruction is occurring as well. For the moment, let us focus on how to ensure that cell phones are not used during tests.

Like most things in teaching, students need to be taught right from the beginning the place of cell phones and other electronic devices during tests and quizzes. The teacher needs to make it clear on the syllabus how cell phones will be handled during tests.

Here is one plausible solution to the problem of the cell phone. The solution involves asking students to turn off their phones and place them in boxes or on desks placed in front of the class, away from students. To ensure that each student complies, students take turns in their rows to come to the front to place their phones in the boxes.

For this procedure to be successful, the teacher needs to introduce it at the beginning of the school year and use it consistently whenever he or she is giving a test or quiz. It is also very important that the teacher takes time to explain why it is necessary for all students to be separated from their phones during a test. Obvious as it may seem, it does not hurt to mention that cell phones contain a lot of information that a student could use during a test or quiz. It is for that reason that cell phones and electronic devices are not allowed on tests such as the SAT and other standardized examinations.

Other problems with cell phones are that they distract students from the task of focusing on the test; one may also mention the problem of sharing the test or quiz with other students who might be taking the test later.

When a teacher introduces the practice of requiring students to place their phones in a box in front of the class, it is not uncommon for one or two students to refuse to place their phones in the boxes or on the desk in front of the classroom. Some students may claim that they fear their phones would get stolen or that they may forget them. When that happens, the teacher may decide to withhold giving the reluctant students their test papers and calmly explain to them why they need to comply. In the end, usually all students place their phones in the boxes and take the test.

If, however, a student were to adamantly refuse to place his or her phone in the box or desk at the front of the class, a teacher would do well to refrain from making a big scene with such a student; in fact, it would be better to let such a student just sit or read something during the test. There is no good reason why the whole class should be disrupted and the test or quiz not given because one or two students refused to turn in their phones. It is best to address such students at the end of the class, or even better, he or she would call their parents and calmly explain what happened.

In this way, one would ensure that the parents are aware and that such a problem would not occur again in the future; this is one situation in which a phone call would work better than an e-mail, and this is also a situation where the teacher has no choice but to contact the student's parents so that there is no repeat of the conduct in the future.

Another area of difficulty is with regard to students' use of cell phones or other electronic devices during instruction. It does not need to be said that a student cannot simultaneously follow a lesson and use his or her phone. Generally, when a student is checking his or her phone, the attention is completely absolved by that phone. Unfortunately, the student fails to understand what is being taught.

A system needs to be developed for discouraging students from using phones during instruction. If the school district does not have a policy for cell phone use in class, or if the district allows their presence in class, the teacher or the school would need to come up with a policy to restrict phone use in class.

Another way of controlling phone use in class involves the teacher taking the phone of whichever student is seen using a phone during instruction. The teacher may decide to keep the phone for the period of the lesson if it is the first offence. If it is repeated, the teacher may keep the phone until the end of the day. For such a system to work, the teacher needs to mention it clearly in the syllabus at the beginning of the school year.

The practice of confiscating phones also has to be started from the beginning of the school year. The teacher has to take time as he or she is presenting the syllabus to explain why it is to the students' benefit for him or her to seize phones when they are used during class. It would also be beneficial for students to discuss this policy before the teacher starts to implement it.

If a teacher decides to seize students' phones, there has to be a secure locked place where the phones can be stored in the classroom. Cell phones are expensive, and there should be no occasion when a phone goes missing after a teacher confiscated it. The teacher should follow strict procedures of locking up the seized phone immediately on getting it from a student. He or she should refrain from putting it anywhere else in the class except the locked cabinet. Postponing putting it in the locked cabinet after seizing the phone can lead to the unintended consequence of the phone getting stolen, which would lead to an enormous problem for the teacher.

Confiscating phones from students who use them during class is probably the most effective deterrent of students' phone use in class. Once one or two students lose their phones during class, the majority of the students may not attempt to use their phones while instruction is going on; the obvious disadvantage of keeping students' phones is the risk of losing them because some students may steal them. Once a phone goes missing, the enormous financial burden the teacher may have to shoulder makes this method of controlling students' phone use in class very risky.

In addition, before a teacher starts to seize students' phones, it would be immensely beneficial for the teacher to discuss this with his or her principal and get the administration's support. Without the support of the administration, it is quite unlikely that such a practice would succeed.

Another, albeit less risky, way of controlling students' phone use in class is through the assignment of participation points. A teacher can decide to assign a certain number of participation points to all students daily. Students get to keep all their participation points if they do not use their cell phones or do not behave in ways that disrupt the class. If a student is seen using a cell phone in class, the teacher may decide to deduct a certain number of points for the infraction. If the student repeats this kind of behavior, the teacher should call the student's parents to inform them and seek their assistance.

Often, the parents' interventions bring to an end such infractions. When they do not, the teacher may continue to deduct points with the knowledge that the student's parents are quite aware of their child's loss of participation points because of his or her phone use in class. Sometimes, that is all the teacher can do when parents do not exert much influence on their children.

Yet another method that some teachers have used to control students' phone use in class has been to ask students to volunteer to surrender their phones if they have difficulties exercising control on their use in class. This practice assumes a great deal of maturity on the part of the student; very few students will voluntarily surrender their phones to the teacher. Most students seem addicted to their phones and cannot part with them unless compelled to.

The unfortunate reality, however, is that students are unable to learn at the same time that they are checking their phones to read and send messages. Each teacher has to find a way of making sure that students are not distracted by their phones and other electronic devices as he or she is teaching. The extent to which a teacher is able to eliminate the distractions presented by phones and other electronic devices may determine how successful he or she is able to teach.

HANDLING STUDENTS' REQUESTS TO LEAVE THE CLASSROOM

Granting students permission to leave the classroom for a variety of reasons is one area that can be a source of conflict. Most students' requests to leave the classroom involve the bathroom. For any teacher, bathroom requests can present a challenge concerning when to write a pass for a student to leave the class. In order to minimize bathroom requests, which some students use to avoid lessons, some schools have a policy that forbids bathroom requests during the first fifteen and the last fifteen minutes of class time.

If such a policy exists, it is a good idea to use it because it helps the teacher refuse to issue a pass during those times and gains the class thirty minutes of uninterrupted instruction. Notwithstanding such a rule, the teacher will still have to decide on who goes to the bathroom for the rest of the class time.

Bathroom requests interrupt instruction and can be a source of disruption if not handled well. A teacher needs to communicate to his or her students that getting permission to go to the bathroom is not something that will be automatically given in order to eliminate frivolous and excessive bathroom requests. The first place to mention this is in the syllabus. It is important to encourage students to use the bathroom as they are transitioning from one class to another.

Using the bathroom at such times minimizes or eliminates the need for most students to ask for a bathroom pass during class. In turn, a reduction in bathroom passes ensures that students benefit fully from what is taught in class because there are minimal disruptions to learning as a result. Like everything else that is important in any class, the fact that it is mentioned on the first day as part of the syllabus does not mean students have learned how to deal with bathroom matters.

A teacher may need to spend a month or more on teaching students about using the bathroom before class. Occasions to repeat instruction on bathroom use may present themselves whenever a student asks for a bathroom pass. As a teacher writes a pass, he or she might remind the student to use the bathroom as he or she transitions from one class to another to avoid having to want to use the bathroom during class.

The teacher must be mindful of not using an accusatory tone, but repeat the expectation in a calm and pleasant fashion so that the student does not feel offended. Other students hear this and also learn that they need to use the bathroom during the transition from other classes.

Generally, most of the students will adjust to the expectation that they will not automatically be granted a bathroom pass whenever they ask for one. There is one important exception, however, to a teacher's attempts at discouraging students from using bathroom requests a lot. This is in the case of an emergency.

EMERGENCY BATHROOM REQUESTS AND REQUESTS TO THE NURSE'S OFFICE

If a student makes an emergency bathroom request, the teacher should always grant one and, at the same time, take note of the fact that such and such a student has asked for an emergency bathroom request. While a teacher should always give permission to leave the classroom to a student who makes an emergency bathroom request, he or she should also explain that these emergencies are not expected to occur to the same person every day. If a teacher notices that the same student is asking for emergency bathroom requests several times a week, he or she should have a private conversation with the student to find out if there is a medical reason for them.

If none seems to exist, the teacher should ask the student to refrain from using emergency reasons for ordinary bathroom requests. In most cases, students will discontinue creating frivolous emergencies. Where the teacher does not see any positive changes, he or she should contact the student's parents to make them aware of the problem and ask for their assistance. Most instances of excessive emergency bathroom requests will end when the parents are involved.

In the event that the parents do not have a lot of influence on their child and he or she continues to make excessive bathroom requests, placing a condition, such as the completion of an assignment as a prerequisite for giving a student a pass for the bathroom, often discourages the unmotivated students to use bathroom breaks to avoid class. This works well with those students who want to avoid class time by spending time in the hallways and the bathroom.

One other request that a teacher should always allow a student to leave class for is the health room or nurse's office. A teacher should never ever deny a student's request to visit the health room unless there is a situation that would compromise the safety of the student if he or she were allowed to leave the classroom at that instant. Otherwise perfectly healthy looking students may have health conditions unknown to the teacher for which they may need to go to the health room.

If a teacher suspects that a student is using the nurse's office to avoid time in class, he or she can do two of the following things. He or she can call the health room after the class period to find out if the student who asked for a health room pass did actually end up visiting the health room. If the answer is in the affirmative, the teacher may ask the nurse whether this particular student will need to be coming to the health room frequently. The nurse may give this kind of information without disclosing private information about the student's health condition.

The second way to handle excessive health room requests is to call parents. This becomes necessary especially if the student does not actually visit the health room on getting a pass from class to do so. Once parents are informed, the problem often disappears. If, on the other hand, the student has a legitimate reason to visit the nurse frequently, now the teacher knows about it.

In some cases where a student has to go to the health room frequently, the nurse may make a permanent pass for such a student so that he or she can leave class whenever the need arises.

KEY IDEAS IN THIS CHAPTER

- Teachers need to arrange desks and other furniture to allow them to reach each and every student quickly and easily in their classrooms.
- Classroom decorations that are attractive show students that a teacher cares about their learning environment and their learning.
- Seating charts need to be ready on the first day of school.
- Class syllabi should contain all the important class information and should be handed out on the first day of school.
- Teachers need to be prepared to teach class routines and expectations over many weeks, sometimes even months. Patience is a critical characteristic to have for teachers to be successful in establishing an environment in which students feel safe to make mistakes and learn without feeling resentful of what the teacher expects of them.

REFLECTION QUESTIONS

1. Mention several things that a teacher needs to do to prepare for students before school starts. What role does getting such things in place play to successful classroom management?
2. How critical is having a seating chart ready before school to a teacher's ability to manage students' behavior right on the first day of school?
3. What four ways of dealing with students' electronic devices are suggested in this chapter? What are the advantages and disadvantages of each of the four ways? What other methods of handling students' electronic devices do you suggest? Explain their advantages and disadvantages.
4. How do you plan to handle students' ubiquitous phones this year?

NOTES

1. Wong, H., & Wong, R. (1991). *The first days of school: How to be an effective teacher.* Mountain View, CA: Harry K. Wong Publications.

Chapter Two

Lesson Preparation and Pacing

OBJECTIVES

1. Teachers will learn how lesson preparation contributes to good class-room management.
2. Teachers will learn effective pacing and its role in good classroom management.
3. Teachers will learn how to effectively use online grade posting portals.

LESSON PREPARATION

Lesson preparation is one of the most important tools in managing a class-room. Before students enter your classroom each and every day, you should know clearly what they will learn on that day and how the process of learning that material will occur. Lack of preparation unfailingly leads to disastrous lessons, with students taking over the class and the teacher experiencing loss of control. The time you spend on preparation depends on several factors.

New teachers, for example, need to spend a lot of time reading what their students will learn to become completely familiar with the content and to anticipate areas that students will have difficulties with. New teachers also need to plan thoroughly all the stages of their lessons and adhere to the lesson plans fully. Due to lack of experience with the unpredictable aspects of classrooms, it is necessary for new teachers to adhere closely to the lesson plan to ensure that

• all the components of the lesson plans are fully covered,

- the pacing of the lessons reflects the well-thought-out plans they made, and
- the lessons follow the sequence that the teachers thought were most logical when they were written.

For new teachers, such detailed lesson plans showing the introduction, lesson development, whole group activities, individualized activities, assessment, and closure should be written the evening or night before the lesson is taught. New teachers need enough time to think about what would work and how to sequence the material to be learned.

Experienced teachers may not need a whole evening to plan a lesson, but even they do need ten to fifteen minutes to write notes in the daily lesson planner what they plan to teach and how the material will be sequenced. Jotting down such notes also enables experienced teachers to remember assignments they need to collect, tests they need to announce, and other important details that they would not think about without a few minutes of reflection about what they anticipate teaching.

In short, both experienced and new teachers need to prepare for their lessons to avoid finding themselves in situations in which they look lost and are attempting to come up with an activity in the middle of a lesson.

CONSEQUENCES OF INADEQUATE PREPARATION

Some obvious pitfalls of inadequate preparation are attempts by a teacher to find material to fill up the remaining twenty-five or thirty minutes left of class time. The stress of the situation can force a teacher to grasp at anything, including the Internet, where there are a lot of unvetted resources. For example, maybe the lesson has been about a chapter in a novel, such as Zora Neal Hurston's *Their Eyes Were Watching God*. Fearing what to do with thirty-something students waiting for the teacher to give them something to fill up the time, the teacher may find a movie on the Internet that seems relevant to what he or she has been teaching.

The teacher tells the class that the remaining class time will be used to reinforce what they have just learned through a short movie found online. The teacher turns out the lights and closes the blinds. The classroom is pitch black, and students sit back ready to watch the relevant clip on the chapter in the novel. The teacher clicks on the play button. As the movie starts, the teacher and the class notice that there are some advertisements. Because *Their Eyes Were Watching God* is a love story, a perverted individual has placed advertisements that are sexually explicit and unquestionably inappropriate for students.

The teacher panics, stops the movie, and apologizes to the class, but the damage has already been done. Some students cheer the teacher on; others are deeply offended, and the teacher has lost credibility with his or her students. Invariably, the story reaches parents, some of whom call the principal to complain. The teacher is summoned by the principal and disciplined for lack of good judgment. He or she apologizes again, but the perception by the principal and parents is that this teacher has poor judgment. This is the kind of mistake that could easily lead to a teacher losing his or her job, and all because he or she failed to prepare.

Other consequences of failure to prepare may not be as devastating as the foregoing one. Nonetheless, they can still lead to unfavorable effects on a class. For example, a teacher may decide on the spur of the moment to do an exercise to fill up the time. Because he or she has not had time to review the exercise, there may be items in the exercise that are not well written that he or she may not be aware of, or the exercise itself may be too difficult or too easy for the students.

If it is too difficult, it can lead to class disruption as students struggle to understand what is beyond them and for which the teacher has not prepared. The teacher himself or herself may seem confused and frustrated and even angry as he or she attempts to understand, for the first time, an exercise that has already been given to his or her students. In short, lack of preparation can lead to chaos ensuing in any class because there is a clear lack of authority when a teacher attempts, in the middle of a lesson, to both teach and understand the material he or she is supposed to teach; students quickly know when a teacher is unprepared and often take advantage of it to sow disruption.

PACING

Effective teachers know that beginning the lesson promptly enables them to gain the class's attention and thus eliminates right from the beginning any disruptive behaviors. The sense that there is no time to waste, because there is indeed never enough time for any lesson, is conveyed to the class when the teacher starts the lesson on the bell. Some students who might have felt the desire to talk do not do so as they notice their classmates turning to the pages of the textbook that the teacher has told them and that the teacher has already begun to make references to.

Any time a teacher refers students to a page, it is always a good idea to write the page number on the chalkboard for three reasons. First, some students may have missed the information about the page and would be assisted by the written information on the chalkboard, and, second, other students need both verbal and written information for them to understand what the teacher is saying. Finally, the teacher saves himself or herself a lot of repetition if the information is also written on the chalkboard.

Often, the beginning of the lesson might involve a ten- to fifteen-minute explanation of new material by the teacher. The explanation needs to have several examples that illustrate what the teacher wants the students to learn. This may be followed by other examples that the teacher uses to ensure that the students are beginning to understand the new concept. At this point in the learning, it is very likely that students would make a lot of mistakes. Some of these mistakes provide the teacher with the opportunity to explain and illustrate further the concept he or she has introduced.

The lesson might then be followed by an exercise that allows students to grapple further with the new concept.

USING FORESHADOWING TO ILLUSTRATE PACING

To make it more concrete, a teacher may introduce the idea of foreshadowing as a literary concept. He or she may give several examples of statements that foreshadow from a reading that the students have already done. At this point, it may be useful to take students to various pages where an author of a particular story provides hints that anticipate a certain event in the story. Having identified several cases like this, the teacher may then tell students to read a short piece of fiction that can be read in, for example, ten to fifteen minutes that has several examples of foreshadowing.

Working individually or in groups, the teacher would tell students to identify examples of foreshadowing that they notice. At the end of the allotted time, as a class, students would then share examples of foreshadowing that they had found in the reading. At this stage, discussions would follow, with the teacher acting as the final arbiter on whether some students' examples of foreshadowing meet the criteria or not.

The sense of purpose and urgency that the teacher sets from the beginning of the lesson has to be sustained in the whole lesson. There are several ways to accomplish this.

First, the teacher has to be keenly aware of where the majority of the class is whenever he or she assigns an activity. When the majority of the class has completed an activity, the teacher must make sure that they promptly move on to the next activity. If students are working individually, the teacher has to move around to monitor how they are performing and where most students are. Obviously, students who need extra time have to be allowed to continue working on an activity while the rest of the class has moved on to the next activity.

At the same time, gifted students who successfully finish activities before most of the class should be allowed to move on to other activities or assigned more challenging work while the rest of the class is completing an activity that the gifted students have already done. A word of caution might be in order here. Experienced teachers know that students who finish assignments before others may not necessarily have done those activities well.

In fact, in every class, there appears to be one or two students who tend to be among the first to finish but produce mediocre work and rush through assignments because they just want to be done with them. For such students, the teacher would need to check the work and ask them to do it again more conscientiously.

A second way of sustaining a good pace in a lesson is through assigning time for activities. The time assigned for a reading, for example, needs to be realistic enough so that the majority of the class can finish the reading in the time allotted. At the end of the allowed time, the teacher may announce that the class is ready to do the next activity. While most of the students may finish the activities within the allotted time, the teacher should be flexible enough to allow the slow workers to continue to work beyond the allowed duration.

Those who finish early can either be assigned other work or be required to wait quietly or take out a novel or any reading to read while waiting for everyone else to finish. It is always a good idea to encourage students to bring their own novels or other types of literature of their liking to class. Whenever they finish work and have idle time, they should be encouraged to take out their favorite literature to read. At no time should students be allowed to just sit and stare into space or put their heads on their desks. Such behavior encourages idleness and the desire to rush through work.

Due to the fact that maintaining a suitable pace throughout the lesson is so critical to managing student behavior, teachers have to constantly monitor what their students are doing in their classes. The arrangement of the desks in the class has to enable the teacher to reach any student easily within the class. Furniture or backpacks should never hamper the teacher's access to any student in the class.

Second, teachers cannot allow themselves to be distracted by e-mails, the Internet, text messages, or anything that compels the teacher to not focus on his or her class as the lesson unfolds. Reading and responding to e-mails should be reserved for planning periods or after school. Teachers who lose focus of their classes due to reading and responding to e-mails or visiting websites pay dearly in student disruptive behavior.

For example, as a teacher is reading an email message or website, a student may throw a tiny piece of paper at another student. The teacher misses the event because he or she is preoccupied with an e-mail or website. Next, there is a broken pencil that is thrown back in response and then a chuckle that the teacher still misses. By the time the teacher notices that there is a paper-throwing fight going on, half the class may be involved, and there may be such a commotion that the teacher may have to resort to yelling and screaming to regain peace in the class.

If such events occur often, the class may promptly descend into an inferno of screaming and out-of-control students and present a severe classroom management problem for the teacher. In turn, the teacher may characterize the class as difficult when, in fact, it is her or his own negligent behavior that lay the seeds for the class's behavioral problems. In short, during a lesson, the teacher's attention should be completely taken up by teaching and monitoring students' performance and behavior. The results invariably lead to well-managed classrooms and students who benefit maximally from the learning activities presented to them.

While moving promptly from one activity to the next and eliminating idle time support a learning environment in which disruptive behaviors are minimized or nonexistent, the manner in which a class ends is also quite an important part of the lesson.

LESSON CLOSURE IS ALSO IMPORTANT

The teacher has to be aware of the time available for his or her lesson and what can realistically be done in the time left. A good closure to a lesson provides students with the opportunity to briefly review what they have learned and enables the teacher to suggest to the class what is to follow. Some good teachers use closure time to ask questions that check for understanding of the salient points of the day's lesson.

Others use closure to give a short quiz or ask some students to give summaries of the main points of the lesson. However closure is handled, it is important that each lesson has a smooth closure to what the students have learned. It may also be during closure that some teachers assign the day's homework.

When a teacher assigns homework, clearly it should be related to the lesson the students have just learned; the homework should provide further opportunities for students to deepen their understanding of the work done in class. Homework that has no connection to the current lesson and is just assigned because the teacher feels that students have to have homework may not do anyone any good. Students may perceive such work as just work for work's sake. Worse still, some students may see it as a form of punishment. Homework, which is an opportunity for students to deepen their knowledge on a topic studied in class, cannot and should never be presented as a form of punishment.

To make it easy and predictable for students, homework may be written in a designated homework section of the class. If the class has enough chalkboard space, there could be one area where homework for various classes is always written. Such an arrangement eliminates the possibility of some students incorrectly copying the homework; it may also serve as a reminder for both the teacher and the students of what the last class's homework was. For absent students, homework written in a designated homework area of the classroom tells them what they missed during their absence.

In any case, if a student claims that he or she did not know what the homework was, the teacher can just point his or her finger at the homework on the chalkboard. Writing homework in a dedicated area of the chalkboard is particularly useful when responding to some students who pretend that they did not know that they had to do three pieces of assignments for homework. When a teacher hears such comments, he or she may just point to the chalkboard and tell the concerned student to read and copy more accurately next time.

TECHNOLOGY AS AN AID TO LESSONS

With good reasons, teachers want to include technology to promote learning. No matter what the circumstances are, never venture into attempting to include technology without having tried it out first during your planning period. As a teacher or student, you have certainly witnessed many occasions when a presenter has struggled with technology.

There was, for example, a principal whose topic of presentation to her entire staff of close to two hundred teachers was about effective lessons. But she herself, having not tried her equipment before the presentation, spent a sweaty twenty minutes unsuccessfully trying to enlarge the size of her visuals on a screen for her entire staff to see. In frustration, she gave up and proceeded to talk about effective teaching while making reference to visuals that nobody could see. She definitely had not tried to use the technology before the presentation and was humiliated by it.

If she had tried the technology the day before, or hours before her presentation, she would have found out that enlarging the images was problematic and would either have sought assistance or found another way of doing it. Once she was in front of her attentive audience, it was too late to find a solution. You do not want to be in such a situation in front of your captive students.

Even simple things, such as videos and CDs, need to be tried out before being shown to a class. Obviously, the video needs to be rewound to where the teacher wants it to begin so that it is ready to show when the teacher pushes play. Easy to operate as a video showing may be, so many things could go wrong if you do not prepare. For instance, you could open the video box and find that the video is not there, or it is damaged, or the video recorder or the TV is malfunctioning, or the cable connecting the recorder to the TV is missing.

To be brief, if you plan to use technology, such as video showing, make sure you have tried it out before class. Do not decide on the spur of the moment that it is a great idea to show a video and then start looking for it as your class watches you. After five minutes or less, the class loses interest and starts to talk while you are furiously trying to show something that you have no idea how it will work because you have not prepared for it.

Other forms of technology that are more complex and unpredictable need thorough preparation. For example, if you would like to show your class something from the Internet, you have to make sure that you can access it and that it is suitable for your class. With material from the Internet and other sources that are not vetted by your school system, you have to be extra careful to ensure that what students see does not offend anyone. Material may be objectionable for a variety of reasons.

Beware that you are answerable for what students are exposed to in your class. Therefore, you have to be doubly certain that what you show them relates to instruction and can be defended on that basis.

Bearing in mind the degree of caution we need to exercise with regard to including technology in our lessons, it is, nonetheless, always a great idea to find ways of enhancing lessons with appropriate uses of technology. Visuals immensely augment oral presentations of material and introduce variety to the lesson; effective teachers always strive to enrich their lessons through technology.

POSTING GRADES ONLINE

Online grade posting is another area where technology clearly helps teachers. This enhanced form of communicating with students and parents has the obvious advantage of keeping students informed about their standing in a course on a regular basis. For teachers who regularly update their grades on the online platform, this method of posting grades can work to their advantage and substantially reduce the need for students and parents to contact teachers about grades. Online grade posting enables parents to monitor closely the performance of their children in a given class.

Most online portals also allow teachers to make comments. For instance, a teacher may be able to indicate why a student did not do particularly well on a quiz or test or received a zero or did not turn in an assignment. These kinds of comments provide parents or guardians with insights concerning why their children may not be doing well in a given course. Teachers who take time to write such comments may obviate e-mails and phone calls from parents or guardians asking about why their children are failing a class.

CONSEQUENCES OF FAILURE TO UPDATE AN ONLINE GRADE PORTAL

One unintended disadvantage of posting grades online is that sometimes students and their parents may have a totally wrong view of their children's standing in a class. This often arises when a teacher fails to update his or her grades for long periods of time. For example, a student may turn in two or three homework assignments and earn full points on two or three quizzes at the beginning of a grading period, all of which a teacher enters on the online portal. On the basis of such assignments and tests, a student's grade may be a 95 percent or even 100 percent.

After such a burst of energy at the beginning of a quarter or semester, the student may decide that he or she has done enough in the class and start to neglect homework and classwork assignments. He or she may also begin to do very poorly on quizzes and tests. At the same time, the teacher may feel that he or she is too busy to update the online portal on a regular basis. He or she may be giving assignments and tests regularly and recording such grades on pieces of paper, waiting for a time when he or she is less busy to update the online portal. Such a time may not present itself until the end of a grading period.

Between the first three weeks of the quarter or the semester and the end of the grading period, several months may have passed during which the student's grade could have dropped from 100 percent to, let us say, 50 percent. However, the parents or guardians may not have known this because the teacher failed to update the online portal and the uninformed parents or guardians simply assumed that what they saw on the online portal was the accurate grade of their child.

You can image the shock that they would experience on finding out that their child has a failing grade a day or two before the end of a grading period when the teacher has finally found the time to enter ten or thirteen different grades that the child had received on numerous assignments over the course of several months. This level of neglect, while often rare, can lead to anger and serious disagreements between parents and a teacher.

While the teacher might correctly argue in his or her defense that the grades entered late legitimately belonged to the student, one cannot fail to see that the teacher's failure to upgrade the online portal to provide parents information about their child as the quarter or semester went by had seriously put them at an unrepairable disadvantage. If the teacher had updated the online portal on a weekly basis, the parents would have been alerted to their child's failing grades and would have had a chance to address the problem as it unfolded.

In fact, the teacher's failure to upgrade weekly the online portal for posting grades rendered the system totally ineffective. Instead of parents or guardians being aware on a weekly basis how their child was faring in the class, they were kept in the dark and discovered that he or she was failing only a day or two before the end of the grading period when the teacher decided that he or she had time to update the grades.

Such a failure does not help parents, in particular, to be the teacher's partners in supporting the education of their children. This kind of failure nullifies completely the effectiveness of a system of posting grades that can be transparent and a tool for ensuring the success of students.

So, to avoid conflicts arising from not updating online grade portals, it is advisable for teachers to update their grades online as soon as an assignment is done; there should be several grades entered on the online grade platform each week. While posting grades online is one way teachers can constantly communicate with parents, communication as an important aspect of teaching is given its due place in the next chapter.

KEY IDEAS IN THIS CHAPTER

- Lesson preparation plays an important role in classroom management because a prepared teacher knows exactly how the lesson will unfold and anticipates students' difficulties.
- Class time is invaluable. Students need to feel from the teacher's sense of urgency that class time is a precious commodity that has to be utilized fully and not wasted.
- Pacing contributes to classroom management because time within class and during transitions is utilized well.
- Online portals for posting students' grades provide vital information to parents. For them to be fully effective, teachers need to regularly upgrade online grades.

REFLECTION QUESTIONS

1. How does lesson preparation contribute to effective classroom management?
2. Why is pacing such an integral part of good classroom management?
3. Besides informing students about their grades, what other educational goals are fulfilled by the regular updating of online grades?
4. Give an example from your own experience or that of another teacher where the lack of preparation clearly undermined classroom management.

Chapter Three

Communication

OBJECTIVES

1. Teachers will learn about how to effectively and efficiently communicate with parents and students using available technology.
2. Teachers will learn how to avoid making common mistakes in using technology to communicate with parents.

Communication is vital to teaching and should be one of the first things a teacher considers seriously as he or she thinks about his or her classes. In actual fact, most teachers, to their own detriment, resort to establishing the means to communicate with parents only after crises have already occurred. Most principals insist that teachers collect students' phone numbers on the first day of school. Some school districts even create e-mail accounts for all of their students.

Both the phone numbers and students' e-mails point to the importance of creating a system of communication with both parents and students.

One way of ensuring that you have parents' e-mail addresses is through the class syllabus that students receive on the first day of school. Within the syllabus, teachers may require that parents send e-mails with their children's names and class in the message line. Sending an e-mail to the teacher instead of writing it on a piece of paper avoids the problem of illegible handwriting that can lead to misreading the e-mail address. Second, it is much easier to copy and paste an e-mail address that is sent electronically than to write it manually when a parent sends it on a piece of paper.

Therefore, for accuracy and convenience, it is best to ask parents to electronically send their e-mail addresses to you during the first two or three days of school. It is important to get this information promptly at the beginning of the school year because it is a critical part of getting your class ready. If you give parents a deadline for when the e-mails have to be done, you are likely to get most of the e-mails by the deadline.

If you do not give a deadline, some parents may postpone sending you the information until you feel frustrated with them. Give parents a deadline for sending e-mail addresses, and you will discover that most of them will meet the deadline.

CREATE A SYSTEM FOR STORING PARENTS' E-MAIL ADDRESSES

Once you have received the e-mail addresses, you may create a digital class contact folder for each class. In other words, for each class that you teach, you create a class contact folder with the students' names and their parents' e-mail addresses. You can use this class contact folder when you need to send an e-mail message to all parents and students in a particular class.

The folder is also useful when you need to reach an individual student because you can always open it to find out about a student's contact information. Both reaching the whole class with one click of a button or contacting one student seems particularly useful at the beginning of the school year when students are learning to adjust to your classes.

First, at the beginning of the school year, it is especially useful to inform parents about important tests, projects, and other class-related matters. The easiest way to do this is through a mass e-mail that reaches all the parents.

Imagine if one were to try to contact all the parents of one's students through the phone! Clearly, it would be a futile exercise and would easily consume eight weeks by the time one had spoken to 180 parents. With an e-mail, the same exercise may take fifteen minutes to compose and send the e-mail.

The second reason why a teacher may need to reach parents easily at the beginning of the school is because she or he wants to make sure that students complete all homework and classwork. If a student is missing any one of the assignments, a teacher may use e-mail to quickly inform parents so that corrective actions can be taken immediately; a brief e-mail that simply says that so and so did not turn in his or her homework would alert a parent and put a stop to a habit that undermines a lot of students' grades.

Furthermore, if a student is showing a tendency to misbehave, a brief e-mail to parents might correct the behavior. E-mails afford teachers an infinitely easy opportunity to reach parents, who are a teacher's most important resource in the education of their children.

Unlike phone calls, which most teachers feel have to be done at school using the school phone for fear that parents and students may have access to their private phone numbers if they make such calls at home, e-mails can be written anywhere. Therefore, even when you feel there is no time at school to send an e-mail, you can take care of that e-mail at home after dinner or even during a weekend.

Because e-mails are so easy to use and do not burden the teacher at all with excessive time demands, teachers should use e-mails to inform parents about such issues as a student's excessive talking, sleeping in class, frequent lateness to class, poor grades, lack of adequate materials, inattentiveness, good class participation, good performance on tests and quizzes, or readiness to help. No issue is too unimportant to inform a parent.

Critical to the effectiveness of e-mail use is to make sure that you accurately collect all your students' parents' e-mail addresses at the beginning of the school year and create digital class contact folders that allow you to send an e-mail with one click of a button to all students in a given class. But in these class contact folders, you can also store students' phone numbers, which you can always access if need be.

CAUTION ABOUT E-MAILS

While e-mails provide the easiest way to contact parents, e-mail messages are also prone to being easily misunderstood. Therefore, a teacher needs to be extra careful when writing an e-mail, particularly if the e-mail is a complaint about a student's behavior. It is not a good idea, for example, to write an e-mail about a student's misconduct when you are feeling angry about what the student did.

Remember that you are writing a parent who loves that child and might be anguished to hear that his or her son or daughter is not behaving well. Most parents feel disappointed when they learn of their children's misconduct, and as a teacher, you have to take those feelings into account as you compose your e-mail message.

Thus, it is always a good idea to write such an e-mail when you have calmed down and can write objectively about the event. In fact, it is advisable that events that cause you to be upset with a student should be told to the parent by phone; the e-mail may not be the better mode of communication for such events. But even when you do decide to call the parent about a situation that made you angry, it is better to wait until you are not upset to make the call.

It is also a good idea to remind yourself that you are not calling to condemn the child, but to seek assistance from the parents so that such behavior does not occur again in the future. Consequently, your call should focus on seeking assistance from the parent to prevent the misbehavior from recurring.

When you call a parent or guardian, use a calm voice and make sure to listen, without interrupting, to what the parent or guardian has to say. Always find something positive to say about the child, and seek the parent's or guardian's help. Refrain from condemning the child, and always sound optimistic about what can be done. Remember that you are the professional and whatever you say about that child carries significant weight. Your statements about the child are comparable to what a doctor says to a patient in his or her office.

MANAGING PARENTS' COMMUNICATION

How and when a teacher responds to a parent's phone call or e-mail has serious implications on the way the teacher is regarded by a parent. To the extent possible, a parent's phone call should be answered as soon as possible, preferably within a few hours of receiving it or the next day. Unless a teacher is absent, days should not pass before a teacher responds to a parent's phone message or e-mail. Understandably, parents get upset when teachers do not respond to their phone messages and they have to resort to contacting the principal in order to get teachers to call back.

Due to the fact that it is easy to read and forget to respond to an e-mail, teachers need to pay special attention to replying to e-mails. One way of doing this is to read e-mails only when one can reply to them; in other words, one can read e-mails only during planning or after school. During such time, a teacher compels herself or himself to reply immediately to all e-mails that require replies. She or he decides that there is no postponing replies and all answers have to be provided there and then. Done in this way, a teacher may discover that he or she never misses replying to e-mails.

However, if a teacher happens to be interrupted by something while reading an e-mail or discovers that there is something more important to do than reading and responding to e-mails, he or she may decide to remind himself or herself about the e-mails that have to be answered the following day. One may place such a reminder visibly on one's desk and make sure that it is the first thing one attends to the following day during planning.

There may be other ways of handling parents' phone calls and e-mails. What is important, however, is that teachers reply to parents' concerns as soon as they receive them. Making parents wait for two to three days worsens their anxieties, and their frustration with the teacher can lead to ugly confrontations.

USING GRADE SHEETS FOR EFFECTIVE
PARENT–TEACHER CONFERENCES

Grade sheets should play a critical role in parent–teacher meetings. Often, potentially contentious parent–teacher conferences can turn out fine because the grade sheet, and not the teacher or the parent or the child, provides an objective document that reveals the student's performance in a given class.

Here is an example of the role a grade sheet played in one teacher's interactions with a parent. For perhaps two or three weeks, a teacher had been receiving lengthy e-mails from parents of a child he had in his class who were arguing that it was not fair to lower the grade of their child because she had turned in an assignment late without a good reason. The parents were expressing their dismay that their child's outstanding grade had been adversely affected by the teacher's act of lowering her project grade by 50 percent.

The teacher had written back to explain that, when a child missed a deadline without a valid reason, the consequence was a 50 percent reduction in the grade that the project would have received.

The parents wrote back to argue that their child was an exemplary student who was contributing so much to the school in the form of, for example, her spectacular performances in sports. As the e-mails flowed back and forth, one of the parents requested to talk to the principal, who was aware of the issue because she had been copied on all the e-mails. The principal spent an hour explaining to the parent that the teacher had made the right decision and that their child's absence, which led to the work being turned in late, was a serious violation of school policy.

After the meeting with the principal, the mother of the child scheduled a meeting with the teacher to discuss the child's grade in the course. Anticipating that the meeting would be a difficult one, the teacher invited one of the guidance counselors to the meeting.

When the meeting began, the parent started by complaining about comments made on one of the essays, but very quickly changed and began talking about how her child had a low grade in this teacher's course because of the low project grade that she had received for having missed a deadline for turning it in. The teacher pointed out that he did not think that 88 percent was a low grade in the course. The mother seemed taken aback and so was the guidance counselor.

She retorted that with a low grade on the project, she expected her daughter's grade to be low. The teacher said that it did not necessarily follow because the project was worth only twenty points. Then, the teacher asked the mother if she had checked her daughter's grades online.

It became obvious that the mother had not been checking her daughter's grades on the online portal and simply assumed that her grade would be very low because of the loss of points on the project that was presented late. When the mother and the guidance counselor saw the grade sheet, the heated argument fizzled away, and the meeting came to an end.

The grade sheet effectively rendered pointless the protracted lengthy e-mails and the conference. While not every parent–teacher meeting is going to be resolved quickly with a grade sheet, it is noteworthy that discussing a student's work without a grade sheet robs the meeting of the most important document in any parent–teacher meeting.

The lesson is very simple: whenever there is a parent–teacher conference, bring a grade sheet for the concerned student. Grade sheets speak for themselves regarding whether or not a child is meeting the requirements of your class. It is for this reason, among others, that your grades should be updated regularly, preferably weekly.

While the foregoing conference was unusual because it was preceded by a plethora of e-mails and a conference with the principal, most conferences happen without prior e-mail exchanges and the expectation that they would be difficult. Therefore, it is tempting for a teacher to trivialize a conference and go in without much preparation.

To be safe, it is best to consider each conference very important and to prepare adequately for it. For each conference, the teacher has to invariably bring a grade sheet and attendance record. The two pieces of information reveal a great deal about a student.

Besides the fact that a student has a certain grade, grade sheets show how the child is performing on quizzes and tests and whether or not he or she is completing most of the assignments. If there are any gaps with respect to work completion, the conference would attempt to find answers for that. Similarly, if the student's record reveals a lot of unexplained absences or lateness, the conference is the right place to address that. Thus, always bring a grade sheet to a conference.

Remember that the raison d'être for a school is learning and grade sheets are the tools that convey that information and should, therefore, be available at any parent–teacher conference.

A parent–teacher conference affords teachers the opportunity to get acquainted with parents and solicit their help if there are problems with a child. Consequently, teachers need to be especially careful not to make a bad impression on the parents. One way of doing this is to listen attentively to what parents are saying and to never interrupt. To the extent possible, teachers should attempt to accommodate reasonable requests that parents make.

For example, if a parent requests that her child's seat be moved to the front of the classroom, there is no need to present an argument against such a request unless there is a possibility that the child might not benefit from such a change. On the other hand, if a parent requests daily or weekly e-mails on her child's progress, teachers should not feel compelled to agree to such a request because it is unlikely that they would be met. In addition, such information might already be available to the parent through the website where grades are posted.

If a parent appears angry, the more reason for the teacher to be calm. An inner voice needs to remind the teacher that he or she can make logical arguments only when he or she is calm. While it might be tempting to get angry also, ultimately, the winner is not the one who loses control but the one who stays calm and rational.

In all encounters with parents and children, teachers need to exercise self-restraint. It is one of the most important character traits that enables good teachers to survive in one of the most challenging professions in the United States.

If a child is not doing well, be prepared that some parents will blame you for the failures of their children. They might blame the fact that you give too many tests or your tests are difficult or that the child is not aware of the homework or that you post homework when the class is about to dismiss. This is where your homework website information needs to be given yet again to both the parent and the child. You should also be able to explain the sources of your tests and quizzes; it is always useful to bring a sample of quizzes and tests for everyone to see.

In addition, you might also inform the parents that important tests are announced several days in advance to allow students to study and that such information is also posted on the homework website. The more access to information about the class you provide the children and the parents, the less tenable would their accusations seem.

Be matter-of-fact in the way you present information. Do not use sarcasm or make insinuating remarks that present you as smarter than the parents and their child. The weight of evidence in your favor should eventually persuade the parent that your intention is not to fail their child; to the contrary, the child would be doing better if he or she were doing the work diligently.

KEY IDEAS IN THIS CHAPTER

- Using e-mails, teachers should create a system of communication that enables them to send mass e-mails to all the students that they teach.
- Mass e-mails can be used to inform parents and students of approaching deadlines for projects, important tests, and progress in the classes on relevant topics.
- Teachers can use e-mails to communicate to parents noncontentious matters, such as missing homework and classwork, poor performance on quizzes and tests, and attendance.

• Teachers need to respond to parents' calls and e-mails promptly within a day or two.

REFLECTION QUESTIONS

1. Besides using e-mails, phones, letters, and digital platforms, are there other ways of effectively communicating with parents and guardians that you would like to share?
2. Supposing a parent or guardian does not respond to your e-mails and phone calls about her child, what else would you do to contact such a parent or guardian?
3. When is it not a good idea to send an e-mail about a student? Why? Please explain.

Chapter Four

Sustaining a Classroom Climate of High Expectations

OBJECTIVES

1. Using real classroom examples, teachers will learn how to consistently maintain a classroom environment in which there are high learning expectations for all students.
2. Teachers will learn that high expectations significantly contribute to managing students' behavior.

It is so obvious that stating it seems rather tautological, but classrooms are places where learning is intended to occur. In discussions of classroom management, the central purpose of the classroom sometimes is forgotten as people focus on the arrangement of the "furniture" of classroom management, namely, routines and procedures, spaces between desks, where staplers and pencil sharpeners are placed, when and why to change seats, and other matters of that sort. No matter how skillful a teacher is on the furniture aspects of classroom management, he or she is bound to fail miserably if he or she cannot create a classroom in which there are high expectations for students' learning.

In other words, students should know and see themselves as accomplishing significant learning experiences in the classroom. It is these meaningful and sufficiently challenging learning experiences that ultimately gain the cooperation of each and every child in the class to focus on learning.

But how does a teacher create and sustain a classroom environment of high learning expectations? It is a simple question that goes to the heart of teaching itself.

GOALS FOR A CLASS PROVIDE A YEARLONG FOCUS

First, the teacher needs to have a vision, articulated or not, of what he or she would like the students to achieve by the end of the school year. For example, an English teacher might want all his or her students to write well-constructed essays and read at above grade level by the end of the school year. These are two significant goals for all his or her students to achieve; notice that the goals are not just for some students to achieve but all students.

Similarly, a biology teacher might have the goal of preparing all her students to pass the state's high school examination. Whatever grade a teacher happens to be teaching, it is essential to have a goal for his or her classes. The goal provides a destination toward which the class aims to go.

Let us use the English goal of getting all students to read at grade or above grade level by the end of the year. Clearly, to achieve such a goal requires the mobilization of all resources that may be available to a teacher.

In the first instance, the teacher might want to test his or her students at the beginning of the school year to establish each student's reading level. Such a test would yield very valuable information showing that some students are already reading at above grade level, others at grade level, and some many grades below the grade level. This vital information would prepare the teacher for the challenges that he or she would face in the year.

Knowing that some students are reading at three or four grades below the grade level, for instance, may bring a sense of urgency to a teacher's class. He or she may be anxious to ensure that the weak students grow rapidly within the year he or she has them.

The knowledge may compel the teacher to maximize the use of each lesson, knowing that if students do not take full advantage of the time with him or her, they might leave the class without improving their reading levels. Furthermore, when the concerned teacher meets with parents, he or she may share what is known about a child's reading level to solicit help from parents.

Consequently, each lesson is not just a lesson for such a teacher but an opportunity for his or her students to take yet one more step toward achieving their goal of improving their reading levels. To improve their reading levels, children have to read. In that case, one has to make sure that they are receiving adequate opportunities to read and write.

Therefore, the teacher should always be mindful about what students are reading at any given point in his or her lessons. One way of doing that, for a reading teacher, is to make sure that, each week, there is at least one major reading assignment that requires reading, writing, and vocabulary work.

WEEKLY QUIZZES AND ONE MAJOR TEST EVERY FOUR WEEKS

While just reading is certainly important, one also wants to be sure that the students' quality of understanding improves. After all, reading is not simply letting one's eyes glance over page after page without making sense of what is read. Reading occurs only when the reader interacts with the text to derive some meaning from what is read.

To ensure that students read with understanding, one may be compelled each time students have read a selection to give them a pop quiz. Invariably, the quiz questions do not test interpretation of the material read; such questions may simply test for basic comprehension of the selection.

Testing students after every reading selection might be laborious to the teacher with respect to grading, but it is a very necessary step in establishing whether or not students are focusing sufficiently on their reading to make sense of it.

For such quizzes to affect students' learning, they need to come unannounced, but after every reading selection. As a result, students will very quickly learn that they have to read each selection well and also do well on the quizzes. In this way, the teacher's goal of ensuring that students are not just reading, but reading to the best of their abilities is achieved as well. Once students realize that each reading experience is important and has immediate consequences for their grades, they will adjust and do their reading conscientiously.

Those students who do not take their reading seriously enough will quickly see their grades drop. Thus, within two to three weeks of starting this system at the beginning of the school year, the teacher may want to contact parents of students whose grades on quizzes and homework are low.

To lessen time spent on making such contacts, he or she may use e-mails and, sometimes, paste in the e-mails students' current grade sheets. Ideally, parents are supposed to check their children's grades frequently and should know that their child is not doing well. In practice, a good number of parents are too busy to check their children's grades and need both the e-mail and enclosed grade sheet to awaken them to the reality of their children's standing in the class.

While students may take weekly quizzes on their reading assignments, they may also complete writing assignments on those readings. The writing assignments may consist of answers to questions that force students to delve deeper into analytical questions on the selections. In addition, students may have to produce one or two pages of writing in response to prompts related to the reading.

In short, four interrelated activities may occur each week in an English class, namely, students read a selection of considerable length and complexity, provide written answers on it, take a quiz on the selection, and write a page or two of continuous prose based on the reading. To help students understand the reading, there should always be discussions of the reading, often guided by the questions that students have answered.

After three or four weeks, students may take a major test consisting of three or four reading selections that they have completed. The major test should always be announced to classes several days before it is taken to enable students to review the selections that will be tested. Additionally, mass e-mails may be sent to parents informing them of the upcoming major test and stressing the need for parents to ensure that their children reread the selections that will appear on the test. Similar information may also be posted on the chalkboard in the classroom and on the website where homework assignments are placed.

Getting students to reread the selections, study the vocabulary, and get really acquainted with what will be on the test affords them further opportunities to develop their competencies in reading and writing.

When the test is administered, it should truly be a major test usually consisting of fifty or more items with open-ended, multiple-choice, and essay questions. Such tests, of necessity, should take a whole class period and account for a significant percentage of the students' assessment grades. Since these tests will come regularly after three or four selections have been studied, students would promptly realize that they have to take seriously all the readings that they are assigned in class as classwork and homework.

Parents also would quickly learn that their children have to give the reading classes the most attention because, frequently, their children would have to demonstrate unambiguously what they have learned.

While the example given here stems from a reading class, one notices that it is applicable to any subject area. In mathematics, physics, chemistry, biology, art, history, US government, and indeed any other subject, it is a good idea to give students a major test every three or four weeks to assess their mastery of content. Such tests allow students to demonstrate several times a quarter their understanding of the content; the tests also reveal how effective the teaching has been.

SCANTRON FORMS LESSEN THE BURDEN OF GRADING MULTIPLE-CHOICE QUESTIONS

This level of frequency in testing students may be facilitated, in part, by using Scantron machines to grade the multiple-choice section of the test; most academic departments in grade schools can spend a little on purchasing Scantron forms for their teachers. Such expenses are not trivial because they can make a difference between a teacher's ability to test frequently or not. Knowing that the bulk of tested material will quickly and accurately be scored by a Scantron machine goes a long way in encouraging a teacher to administer a test to all his or her students.

While the essays and the open-ended questions have to be graded by the teacher, it is still a big advantage to have thirty or forty items on a test scored efficiently by a Scantron machine. Furthermore, use of Scantron machines eliminates questionable practices, such as using students to grade each other's work. Such a practice may create the possibility of students conspiring to help each other if they are regularly asked to grade each other's work.

Another advantage of using a Scantron machine to grade some of the work stems from the fact that such grading is perceived as impartial; the notion that such and such a student received a better grade because the teacher likes him or her is ruled out with machine grading.

Notice that because of one's use of the Scantron machines to grade multiple-choice questions, one's time is freed to focus on students' writing while they are simultaneously developing their reading abilities. On the basis of their writing results, one may introduce important components of writing such as thesis statements, introductions, topic sentences, supporting a thesis, transition words and phrases, body paragraphs, and conclusions.

Through reading, therefore, a teacher may simultaneously incorporate writing in his or her lessons. The writing experiences can accompany all the readings that the students do. Almost all reading selections should provide students with opportunities to write. In addition, a teacher may formally teach other types of writing: personal narrative, persuasive, argumentative, and comparison and contrast. Thus, the following three goals of improving reading, comprehension, and writing are met simultaneously. A similar strategy that ensures that several goals are pursued in classroom instruction can be used in any subject area.

Another illustration of simultaneously pursuing several goals can be done, for the reading teacher, in the systematic study of grammar. A good grasp of sentence structure helps students with reading and writing. With writing, in particular, the study of grammar helps students better understand the correct use of tenses; subject–verb agreement; indefinite pronouns as subjects; and simple, complex, and compound–complex sentences, among many other topics.

To cater for the study of grammar, a teacher may devote ten to fifteen minutes in every lesson to grammar. Thus, as the year goes by, students move from parts of speech to phrases, clauses, types of sentences, tenses, agreement, and other aspects of sentence structure. And as students complete each chapter, they also take tests, which reveal their levels of mastery of each chapter.

While assessments are crucial to finding out whether students are making the kind of progress the teacher expects, there are other areas where students can assume some role in their own academic growth. For any teacher, it is important to recognize that students have to be afforded opportunities to develop on their own. In history, such opportunities may be presented to students as research topics. In other words, students are given research topics that they work on with the teacher's supervision. As students gather reading material, read, select relevant information, organize it, and write their papers, undoubtedly, a lot of learning is happening involving many skills, such as reading for comprehension, sorting information and deciding on the best way to present it, and writing in a manner that makes the information accessible to the reader. These are skills that a teacher can help foster in students by giving them research topics to work on.

BOOK REPORTS ARE AN IMPORTANT TOOL FOR DEVELOPING STUDENTS' COMPETENCIES

For an English teacher, the reading for and writing of book reports provide opportunities for students to develop several capabilities on their own. Done well, book reports develop students' vocabulary through exposure to an infinite number of contexts in which words are used normally, awareness of variety in the way to compose effective sentences, and reading comprehension. An English teacher realizes quickly that he or she has to take students on a tour of the school library so that the librarian can explain to them how to use it. During such a visit, students may be introduced, for example, to the idea of biweekly book reports.

The idea is simple. Once every two weeks, students may be taken to the library to return and checkout books. The expectation is that each student completes reading one book during the two-week duration and writes a report on it. How the report is written depends on the teacher's choice. Some teachers use a form with detailed questions that students are asked to answer in complete sentences.

However, what is important is that students truly complete reading a book in the two-week period and write a form of a report on it. Done consistently over a period of a semester, for instance, students' gains in reading and writing can be astronomical.

While students are strongly urged to bring their book report books to class all the time, class time cannot adequately cater to students to do their readings in class. With book reports, the expectation is that students will do the bulk of their reading at home. Therefore, in fact, students assigned to read for book reports have homework assignments daily, which involves reading for forty-five minutes to an hour of their books for book reports.

With respect to class time for the English class used in this example, observe that each lesson has ten to fifteen minutes of grammar and exercises on that. There also has to be time to introduce a reading or do an actual reading (although this may be completed as homework) or grammar related to the reading. Furthermore, students may also use part of class time to read for their book reports, although most of this type of reading may also be done as homework. The lesson may also include some formal writing activity, such as steps to developing an argumentative essay. The class may also have a novel that it is studying together.

In brief there is no idle time in the class because there are numerous activities that demand the students' attention. Thus, classes that are driven by an overwhelming sense of purpose are invariably spared the toxins of class disruptions. The pervading atmosphere of being goal driven does not leave room for the disinterested student to start creating problems for others and the teacher. Ultimately, all the activities are assessed in one form or another, and the results of such assessments find their way into the grade book.

Since most school districts have the capacity to post grades online, parents have easy access to them and most may be constantly aware of how their children are performing. Nonetheless, if a teacher notices that some students are being negligent of homework or classwork or have not been doing well on tests and quizzes, he or she should send a quick e-mail alerting their parents to the fact; for the rare parents who do not use e-mails, a phone call may be in order.

Therefore, working with parents by regularly posting students' grades online where parents have access to them, informing parents about important tests and projects, keeping parents always aware of assigned homework by posting it on the homework website, ensuring that students do their assignments by constantly checking them, and frequently assessing students through quizzes and tests, a teacher can create classrooms in which high academic and behavioral expectations are maintained.

Primarily, the goal of any class should be for students to attain high levels of learning; an effective teacher demands the best of his or her students at the grade level she or he is teaching. A consequence, however, of the pursuit of high academic achievement for each student seems to be that students inevitably focus on learning and have no time to misbehave. As the many facets of a teacher's focus on instruction reach parents and affect students' learning, a teacher my find himself or herself enjoying tremendous support from an overwhelming majority of parents who value the gains their children make in his or her classes.

Sustaining a climate of high academic expectations, of necessity, creates a class climate free of unruly behaviors, where learning occupies the minds of all the students; even the few reluctant learners find themselves unwittingly caught in the positive momentum the majority of the students generate.

It would be misleading to pretend that sustaining high academic expectations does not demand a certain level of commitment from the teacher. Let us address some of the factors a teacher might consider to successfully keep his or her students focused on instruction for the entire school year.

CONCURRENT CONSIDERATIONS

Good teachers know that you cannot teach when some students are talking or being distracted by some activity irrelevant to the lesson. So it is legitimate to ask, how does a teacher pack his or her lesson with so much activity and momentum and, at the same time, take care of the inevitable slight and yet significant perturbations that could also be happening in the class? This section of the chapter addresses these.

The term *concurrent* captures the simultaneity with which a teacher both teaches and nips in the bud behaviors that have the potential to derail a lesson. While teaching and as the majority of the students are engaged in the main business of the lesson, an effective classroom manager continuously monitors the whole class and is able to pick up cues from students suggesting confusion, understanding, questions and lack of attention. He or she uses such information to reteach aspects of the lesson that may be confusing or might decide to ask questions that enable students to give answers that lead to a better grasp of the material.

Such continuous monitoring of the whole class also enables the teacher to stop behaviors that have the potential to escalate and disrupt the lesson. It is this kind of awareness that prompts effective managers to direct simple questions to those they perceive as inattentive. Sometimes, the teacher just moves closer to the student whose behavior is off task; other times, just a sustained gaze at the off-task student gets him or her back. At this stage of student behavior intervention, the teacher's actions do not draw the attention of the class and are intended to allow the lesson to move along without disruption.

These types of actions, which prevent certain inappropriate behaviors from taking root and blossoming into full-blown acts of severe class disruption, account for a great deal in well-managed classes. It is infinitely better for a teacher to prevent an incident of class disruption than to have to address open defiance and rude behavior or a fight in a class.

When an incident escalates to a point where it interferes with every student's ability to learn, at that point the teacher may not really have measures to deal with it within the class. His or her viable option may be to remove the student from the class; removing a student from a class relies on the timely involvement of security or administrators.

In a large school, such timely assistance is never guaranteed, and the disruptive student might continue to linger around the classroom for ten or fifteen minutes capturing the attention of the whole class and making it impossible for the lesson to resume. Thus, classes are much better served when a teacher is able to stop a potential off-task behavior from growing into a huge scene in a class.

An Example of the Importance of Constantly Monitoring a Class

Here is one concrete example illustrating the efficacy of a teacher's constant monitoring of his students.

There was a quiet student at the beginning of the school year who happened to be near a big box full of tissues. As the teacher passed by this student for the first and second time, he noticed that the student was balling tissues and throwing them under some other students' seats; he wanted to create the impression that the students with tissues under their seats had been doing this. The teacher moved the box of tissues to a distant seat and calmly and quietly asked the student to pick up the litter of tissue balls he had created.

There was no incident, and the student quietly complied. If the teacher had not been monitoring his students, you can imagine how much of a mess this student would have created. First, there would have been a whole box of tissues emptied and scattered in balls all over the floor. Second, the number of students affected would have been larger, and that would have created a whole-class incident that would have interfered with the lesson. Third, the teacher would have been quite angry at the level of vandalism if he had discovered the problem when the whole box had been emptied. His constant monitoring of the class helped minimize the damage the student created and lessened the impact it had on the class.

With the availability of laptops and the Internet, it is tempting for teachers to check e-mails and other websites during class time. The major problem with such activities is that they interfere with monitoring what the class is doing, and, thus, the teacher may fail to take preventive actions when they are needed. To be effective class managers, teachers have to always be aware of what every child is doing in their classes. Threats to the tranquility of a classroom are best dealt with when they are just beginning; once they blossom, it is often too late to find anything that would effectively contain them.

Managing Transitions in Classrooms

Another concurrent aspect of instruction in a well-paced classroom and adequately challenging class is the smooth management of transitions. To minimize loss of valuable class time during transitions, it is best for teachers to teach their classes routines about how to handle certain transitions.

For example, if the class routinely changes textbooks in the middle of the lesson and some books have to be put back on the shelf, the teacher has to find a quick and efficient way of enabling the class to perform such an activity. Some teachers might appoint row leaders: students whose responsibility is to carry all the books from their rows and neatly put them on the shelves. Others may have all students in each row taking turns to bring their books to the shelf.

Whatever system the teacher chooses, it has to be smooth and efficient. Teachers have to think about the manner in which daily routine activities will be done in their classes and teach the students how to perform such activities with the least level of disruption to the lessons.

Beginning of Class

Similarly, the beginning of class needs careful consideration to prevent loss of valuable time and the possibility of disruptive behaviors taking root and making it difficult for the teacher to gain control of the class. One way of making sure that students quickly settle in their seats and focus on instruction on the bell is to make the beginning of class predictable. As mentioned before, most teachers begin class with a warm-up activity. The easiest way to gain class control from the moment students enter the class is to have the warm-up activity ready.

Additionally, it also helps to make the way the activity is done predictable; in other words, while the questions for the warm-up may change daily, the manner in which they are done should not require explaining each day. Being predictable with the way things are done in class reduces confusion and enables the majority of students to focus on what is actually new.

Yet another way of encouraging students to settle quickly at the beginning of class is to offer points to students who start their warm-up soon after entering the classroom. The teacher may assign ten or fifteen points to those students who seem to quickly sit and begin their warm-up, even before the tardy bell rings. The points may be considered extra credit for the students who earn them. Such a practice may be done on randomly selected days to compel all students to be on the lookout daily.

The randomness keeps most of them on their good behavior; eventually, the whole class benefits from the fact that the majority of the students transition well at the beginning of class.

The Lesson

Once the warm-up is done, the teacher should punctually begin the lesson. It is also important to make the transition from the warm-up to the main lesson highly predictable to avoid loss of valuable class time and eliminate confusion. It is a good pedagogical practice to follow similar sequences of activities even as the material that a teacher teaches is different.

For example, after the warm-up, a teacher may routinely follow up with a short lesson on a grammatical point, perhaps related to the warm-up itself or to a reading the students have just done or to a writing assignment the students have just completed.

Whatever the topic, the teacher makes his or her lesson predictable to his or her students by doing a brief lesson on grammar; he or she may do this for most of the school year. The point is that students get accustomed to doing some grammar after the warm-up before moving on to the main lesson of the day.

The main lesson of the day may also follow predictable patterns. For instance, if students were assigned a text to read as homework, there may be several possible follow-ups to the reading, such as a quiz, a discussion of the text, a reading of students' short essays on the reading, or a discussion of the vocabulary work on the text.

If students are reading a novel and were assigned a chapter to read as homework, some of the following may be expected: a quiz on the chapter, an analytical discussion of the chapter to help students fully understand the chapter, some vocabulary work, or a short writing assignment related to the reading.

The teacher may also focus on some literary aspects of the text, such as allusions, symbolism, foreshadowing, diction, mood, or the intersection of syntax and meaning. For example, how does the author foreground or background information through the manipulation of syntactic structures, or what is the place of dialect in capturing the veracity of the local idiom in the novel?

In novels such as *Things Fall Apart*, *Their Eyes Were Watching God*, or *Grapes of Wrath*, one clearly sees a lot of opportunities to make students aware of the author's role in capturing local idioms by using the vernacular forms of language or idiomatic expressions.

Chinua Achebe says in *Things Fall Apart*, "Among the Igbo the art of conversation is regarded very highly, and proverbs are the palm-oil with which words are eaten."[1] In this novel, Chinua Achebe invests a lot in the use of proverbs and idiomatic expressions to give the reader a definite Igbo flavor and point of view. Students need assistance in understanding this unique perspective that the novel provides.

End of Class

Besides the beginning of class and between activities within the lesson, another area of transition is the end of class. Ineffective teachers often give the impression that they have run out of material before the end of class, allowing the class to idle and get into serious mischief in the last ten or fifteen minutes of class.

There should be no idle time in a well-paced and consistently demanding class; in fact, students should always feel at the end that they did not have enough time for all the work that was planned for that day. Good class managers often use the last five minutes of class time to review what the lesson has just covered.

With a little preparation, a teacher may ask questions that reveal whether or not students understand the main concepts learned. Notice that it is the teacher who asks questions in this part of the lesson; it is not sufficient to ask if students have questions. Most of the time, students do not even know that they do not understand something. It is, thus, up to the teacher to find out with well-thought-out questions if students understand or not.

Starting the homework is also another profitable way of ending a class, as long as this simply allows students to understand how to do the work and is not intended to occupy a good part of the lesson. Some homework assignments require the teacher's explanations, and it may be useful to students to start such assignments in class. But even if there is no homework to assign or the review of the lesson to be done, there are still other things a teacher may choose to do in the last few minutes of class.

For example, a teacher may decide to prepare the class for the next lesson. Questions or a narrative or a short writing assignment that cultivates interest in the next lesson could be introduced in the last few minutes of class. In short, there should really be no idle time at any point in a class; managing these types of transitions sustains a climate of high academic expectations in classrooms and eliminates the occurrence of misconduct.

MANAGING THE TEACHER'S TIME: QUIZZES

Teaching classes in which every lesson is meaningful and students are afforded numerous opportunities to develop their competencies through classwork, homework, quizzes, tests, writing assignments, and projects demands a great deal of the teacher's time. To succeed in running such classes, a teacher has to think very carefully about how he or she uses planning periods and time outside of the school day.

First, students need to get results of their quizzes, tests, projects, and writing assignments promptly. With regard to quizzes, which may be given weekly, a teacher has to make sure that the questions are few, five or six, but not exceeding ten. Furthermore, quiz questions should focus on such aspects of learning as basic comprehension; the answers to them usually should not require analysis, synthesis, comparison and contrast, or lengthy explanations. As a result, if possible, students should be able to answer quiz questions in a word or phrase. For example, to the question, "Who was the leader of the Bolshevik revolution?" a student may simply write, "Lenin."

It is clearly faster to grade a one- or two-word answer than a whole sentence. These kinds of answers reveal quickly whether the child has read and therefore knows the story or not. With these kinds of quiz responses, a teacher may easily grade one quiz paper a minute and can finish a whole class in half an hour; it might take ten minutes to enter the grades on the online grade portal.

In mathematics, answers to quiz questions might just be the solutions to the problems; whatever the subject, a teacher needs to find a simplified way of quickly finding out if his or her students understand what they have studied. In short, grading quizzes should be an infinitely manageable task and one no teacher should hesitate to do each week for all of his or her classes.

However, while the quiz questions are created to be in such a way that any student who has done the work should score well, they still serve a very important function in the learning process. How a student performs on the quiz questions reveals whether he or she is actually doing his or her assignments. Students who do not read assigned work will perform poorly on quizzes, while those who do read will do well. Such fundamental information is critical to both the teacher and parents.

If a student is failing a class because he or she is not doing classwork and homework as shown by the grades he or she receives on quizzes, the teacher and parents would have to find a way to get such a student to take care of such work.

GRADING WRITING ASSIGNMENTS

Grading writing assignments may be extremely time consuming if not handled properly. One way to make writing assignments manageable is to narrow the focus of each assignment. For example, at the beginning of the school year, the focus may be on writing good topic sentences for each paragraph and developing the argument fully. One might start such a task by getting students to write one or two paragraphs only; grading such pieces is less burdensome than grading five-paragraph essays that are full of many different errors that a teacher may attempt to correct all at once.

Another advantage of giving students narrowly focused writing assignments is that students may also get a sense of achievement when their writing pieces are graded. Because the teacher is not assessing the writing assignment on the basis of other factors, such as tense shifts, run-on sentences, transition expressions, or effective introductions or conclusions, the student may get a good grade on a piece of writing simply because the focused and narrow objective for the writing was met.

This does not suggest that the other factors, such as using tense and transitions effectively, do not matter. It just means that for the present purpose of the writing assignment, the teacher has chosen to focus on what he or she wants the students to master. At the same time, this narrow focus enables the teacher to provide quick and meaningful feedback to students. In turn, the students do not get overwhelmed by what might appear as too many errors in their essays if the teacher comments on everything.

There are two disadvantages with this approach to essay writing: lack of transference of skills by students and fragmentation of the essay-writing experience. Both will be addressed briefly in the following paragraphs.

Lack of Transfer of Skills

Lack of transfer of skills by students relates to the commonly observed fact that students rarely transfer a skill learned in one context to another. In other words, if students learn to write and develop one or two paragraphs in isolation, there is a tendency for them to not apply that learning in another context that might require those skills.

So given a five-paragraph essay that involves writing good topic sentences and developing full arguments related to such topic sentences in subsequent paragraphs, a majority of students may fail to do so even, when in isolation, they were able to show such competence. This lack of transfer of knowledge is a quite well-known phenomenon in studies on students' learning and poses a nontrivial obstacle to approaches to teaching that rely on students' ability to apply knowledge learned in one context to another related context.

One possible way of mitigating the effects of the lack of transfer phenomenon in writing might be to ask students to write full essays of at least five paragraphs even as the teacher's focus in grading them would be on one or two aspects of essay writing. In other words, the teacher may ignore other errors in writing and simply focus on one or two skills and grade students on the basis of the selected skills. In this way, the teacher is not overwhelmed by attempting to correct all errors, and students are made to feel that they have achieved some level of mastery to the extent that they are assessed on one or two skills in an essay.

Another problem worth noting with respect to writing in particular concerns the fragmentation of the writing process. If transitional expressions, thesis statements, introductions, body paragraphs, tenses, agreement, and other aspects of writing are taught in isolation in an approach to essay writing that narrowly focuses on one of these topics at a time, students may lose sight of how in fact all these subtopics are organically interrelated and work together to create a coherent and effective essay.

Thus, given a writing assignment requiring them to use the various aspects of essay writing they learned, students may fail to deploy simultaneously the skills that they mastered in isolation and may produce writing that still reveals a lack of competence in the very same domains where they showed mastery in isolation. It is therefore important to realize that the practice of segmenting and isolating writing skills has its severe limits in the process of developing good writing in students.

Once again, it seems beneficial to students to get them into the habit of writing full five-paragraph essays even when, for purposes of grading and attaining a sense of accomplishment, it is good for the teacher to grade narrowly, focusing on one or two skills involved in essay writing. Done in this way, students are constantly writing full essays that superficially address all aspects of writing, even though their grades and the teacher's comments focus narrowly on one or two skills.

RESEARCH PAPERS

In other subject areas, such as social studies, science, and mathematics, teachers may need to consider how to break down large topics in order to make them accessible to students. Instead of asking students to write a five-page research paper, it might be better to begin with a paragraph and gradually move to a page. Such an approach to research papers may prepare students better for the longer projects and lessen the multitude of errors that students are likely to make.

When, without thorough preparation, students are told to come up with a five-page research paper, it should not be surprising to the teacher that some of them will repeat, ad infinitum, the numerous errors that might frustrate the teacher; these are the kind of errors that could have been addressed and corrected in a smaller sample of writing, perhaps limited to a page.

Ultimately, however, good writing exhibits an awareness of all the various components that have formed the writing exercises that we have discussed above. Thus, at some point, a teacher will require his or her students to write an essay that reflects awareness about tense shifts, subject–verb agreement, effective thesis statement, topics and their development, good introductions and conclusions, transitional words and phrases, and consistency in point of view.

However, even while students are demonstrating their overall awareness of what constitutes a good essay, the teacher may still set limits to the task by asking them to write a five-paragraph essay. Generally, there is not much to be gained in middle and high schools by asking students to write five- or six-page essays, especially if that is done only once during the entire school year. There may be a lot of fear and anxiety that such an exercise generates in the student, but its educational value, with regard to teaching students to write well, is highly dubious.

In contrast, if a teacher can get his or her students to write ten or fifteen short, focused pieces in a year, the students' abilities in writing are likely to improve as they learn from the numerous focused experiences. The many short papers are clearly better than the one long paper that overwhelms both the teacher and the student but is full of errors.

MAIN POINTS OF THIS SECTION

Observe that, for both quizzes and essays, the teacher has to find ways of providing students with prompt feedback by focusing on what each activity is intended to achieve. Quizzes are an efficient and quick way of establishing whether students understand what they have learned. Therefore, to simplify the grading of quizzes, encourage students to answer in a word or phrase.

In contrast, essays are both a way of teaching writing and assessing whether or not students, for example, have developed the capability of bringing together information that makes it accessible to the reader in a coherent manner. If it is an argumentative essay, has the student learned how to take a position, find examples that support it, explain the relevance of those examples to the thesis, and conclude in an effective way?

Has the student presented his or her argument in the most persuasive way? Are word and sentence structure choices reflective of the student's awareness that his or her goal is to persuade the reader? What is the tone of the essay in general?

As can be seen, there are a lot of factors that go into writing an effective essay. Thus, ultimately, a grade assigned to an essay must take into account how all the aspects of the essay work together.

While rubrics that attempt to quantify how points are assigned for an essay are definitely useful and should be used, there is no denying that stylistic factors of the essay, which play a considerable role in an essay's overall impression, are hard to quantify. Nonetheless, a teacher knows when he or she comes across a word or sentence structure choice that works particularly well in a student's essay. Conversely, when a student uses words poorly and writes in structures that do not show awareness of the role of such elements in writing, an effective teacher is turned off and may assign a poor grade to such an essay.

GRADING STUDENTS' PROJECTS

Another area of students' work that often consumes a lot of teachers' time is projects. Generally, projects tend to be lengthy pieces of work and carry more points than regular assignments. Because a single project may encompass many aspects, such as, for example, a map, drawings, narratives, a poem, or pictures, detailed rubrics tend to be very necessary to help students understand how each component of the project is weighted. Rubrics also help the teacher by providing him or her a quasi-objective way of assessing the various parts of the project.

Done well, projects do enrich students' learning and give them an opportunity to exhibit their strengths in areas that are usually not assessed in classes. For instance, a student who is good at drawing and not writing may show her or his ability in drawing through a project and earn a good grade as a result.

Advantages of Presenting a Project

Besides using detailed rubrics to grade projects in a more objective way, teachers can also get students to present their projects and grade them as they are being presented. There are three advantages to presenting projects.

The first advantage is that students are usually motivated to produce good work if they know that other students in the class will get to see it, especially through a presentation to the class; most students do not want to appear in front of other students with a piece of work that is clearly inferior.

The second advantage is that students in the class get to enjoy the variety and differing quality of projects that students in class present. Class presentations can break the monotony of book work in classes.

The third advantage of class presentations is that they do speed up the grading of projects by the teacher. As students present their projects, the teacher can evaluate the projects and assign grades right away. In this way, the teacher does not have to laboriously go through each lengthy project during planning time, reading the written sections, and viewing the drawings and other details. All that type of information could be presented to the class by the concerned students, and the teacher would listen, view the material, and evaluate it.

Thus, using a detailed rubric, the teacher may assign a grade to each project at the end of each student's presentation. Students would then get feedback on their projects as soon as the presentations are completed.

Ensuring Smooth Project Presentations

Notwithstanding the obvious advantages listed above of students' project presentations, one needs to be aware that students' conduct during presentations has to be guaranteed to not disrupt the presentations. Some students are strong presenters and easily command the attention of their peers. Unfortunately, there are also some students whose weak voices, timidity, and even the poor quality of their products may elicit comments, laughter, and disruption to the project presentation.

To avoid such situations from arising and destroying some students' presentations, a teacher has to set some rules about the conduct of the class during presentations. Before presentations are done, a teacher may give the class rules, such as the following:

1. There will be no talking or any disruptive behavior while a student is presenting.
2. Comments or any behavior that disrupts a presentation will lead to a loss of points by the disrupter.
3. At the end of a presentation, we all clap for the presenter and ask questions if there are any.

As a student is presenting, the teacher should be keenly attentive to the presenter and not allow any other student to interfere with the presentation. If he or she notices any student disrupting in any way another students' presentation, a penalty for the disruption in the form of loss of participation points should be communicated to the disrupter while ensuring that the presenter is not further subjected to more disruption.

Ideally, the teacher should simply take note of the disrupter and enter a penalty in his or her grade book. However, if the disruption is clearly interfering with the presentation and making it difficult for other class members to follow, the teacher may decide to address the disrupter so that the presentation can continue smoothly.

The decision concerning what to do with the disrupter will depend on the teacher's knowledge of the student and how he or she is receptive to correction. It is never a good idea to get involved in a discussion with an argumentative student in front of a whole class. For those types of students, it is better to speak to them privately, away from the public gaze of the whole class.

WHY WRITING HOMEWORK AND CLASSWORK IN NOTEBOOKS IS GOOD FOR STUDENTS

In middle and high schools where a single teacher may teach from three to perhaps six different classes a day depending on the kind of schedule a school uses, the issue of how one handles students' assignments is worth some attention. Enabling ninety to two hundred students manage the various assignments that they complete is a serious matter.

To reduce instances in which students lose or claim to lose assignments, a teacher has to come up with a system for how students write assignments and turn them in. As is well known, students frequently misplace or lose assignments written on loose-leaf paper and carried in backpacks. To minimize and even eliminate the possibility of a student losing his or her assignment, it is a good practice to require that classwork and homework assignments be done in two separate notebooks, labeled classwork and homework, respectively. Teachers may insist that students use notebooks to turn in work and not turn in work on loose-leaf paper.

As a result of following this stringent practice, students' work is automatically organized into classwork and homework, and the risk of a student losing one or two assignments is eliminated.

Additionally, when the teacher wants to check for some assignments, he or she just collects a class's notebooks and looks through them for the work that is supposed to be there. If an assignment is missing in a notebook, the teacher writes a brief comment indicating what is missing. If a student is absent, his or her notebook is not going to be in the pile of turned-in notebooks, and the teacher also quickly notes the absence of both the student and the work in his or her grade book.

When there is a conference and there are questions about a student's work habits, the student's notebook acts as a very powerful document that reveals whether or not the student has been doing sufficient work in a class. Notice that it would be extremely challenging to get a student to bring to a conference all the assignments that he or she had done for classwork and homework if those assignments were done on loose-leaf paper. It is very likely that the student would lose most of such assignments two, three, four, five, or six months into the school year.

With notebooks, all the work that a student has done should be in the notebook. If the student produces the notebook, which it is advisable for the teacher to check weekly, it should be apparent to everyone what kind of student he or she is based on the teacher's comments in the notebooks and the kind of grades he or she receives. To truly help both teachers and students, grade school students are best served by the use of notebooks.

But notebooks are also particularly helpful for students who have learning disabilities, such as attention deficit disorder, and other disabilities that manifest themselves in students' lack of organization, forgetfulness, and absent-mindedness. Students of this type immensely benefit from the structure that notebooks provide in terms of where they place assignments.

Instead of the teacher dealing with the endless claims that an assignment was done and forgotten at such and such a place, notebooks compel students to do their work in only one place, and they cannot claim that they did it and just forgot the piece of paper somewhere else.

Obviously, there are other ways of managing students' assignments. For example, with the proliferation of online platforms for posting work, some teachers require their students to post work on some sites that act as safeguards against losing work. But even on such sites, it is important that a teacher thinks through how the assignments will be easily accessed, graded with comments, and be shown as evidence in the event that such information were needed.

Experience shows that asking students to write on loose-leaf paper with the hope that they can keep an organized filing system in which all the assignments are chronologically arranged is unrealistic for most students in grade school; rare is the student in grade school who keeps an organized filing system for his or her assignments.

The point is that each teacher needs to find a system that ensures that students do not lose their completed assignments and that the teacher can find such assignments whenever he or she needs to see them.

MANAGING STUDENTS' PROJECTS AND ESSAYS

Related to the matter of notebooks are long assignments, such as projects and essays. Here, again, a teacher needs to have a system for handling such assignments. It is very discouraging to any student for a teacher to lose a student's work; if such a thing occurs, it should be the exception and not a routine occurrence.

One way of ensuring that students' essays or projects are not misplaced is to create folders in which a teacher places students' work whenever it is received; each folder is for a different class. For example, all essays on a certain topic are paper clipped and placed in a folder for each class that did that assignment.

Second, it certainly helps to grade the work as soon as possible; essays for one class may take a day or two. Promptly getting the work graded and returned to students prevents some of it getting lost. The idea is simple. Due to the fact that the teacher does not allow students' ungraded work to pile up on his or her desk, there is no clutter on the desk, and all assignments are accounted for within a week or two. This clearly contrasts with a situation in which a teacher has a Mount Kilimanjaro pile of students' ungraded assignments.

First, such a sight does not inspire confidence in students or parents that the teacher is capable of handling the work he or she has been giving students. Second, when the teacher, a month and half later, grades one of the assignments and tells a student that his or her work is missing, the child is not likely to remember the assignment in question and might genuinely think that he or she did it. Because of the long period that has elapsed since the work was given, the teacher lacks credibility to insist that the work was not done.

As expected, perhaps, taking too long to grade students' work seriously undermines a teacher's standing and does affect how students respond to the teacher in class. In the first place, students want to know within a reasonable time how they have performed.

Such information is important, especially to those students who prepare well. Promptly providing such feedback to students encourages them to want to work even harder for the next time. It certainly makes a lot of sense for students to receive feedback before they are given another project or essay from the same teacher.

So a crucial part of sustaining a climate of high expectations in a classroom involves students learning quickly the results of their performance on assignments.

ORDERLINESS IN THE CLASSROOM

Another area worth considering with respect to students' assignments relates to orderliness in the areas where students' assignments are kept. Owing to the fact that a lot of papers are generated in regular classrooms, a teacher needs to be particularly vigilant in ensuring that his or her class does not appear hopelessly cluttered with papers.

Periodically, therefore, the teacher has to file or get rid of worthless paper that tends to accumulate on tables and the teacher's desk. Getting rid of such junk helps the teacher to keep track of the important assignment papers that he or she receives from students. Furthermore, the general impression of a free-from-clutter classroom gives students and parents the confidence that their teacher is very much in control and not overwhelmed.

KEY IDEAS IN THIS CHAPTER

• Meaningful learning and well-managed classrooms are related because students' sense that what they learn in class has relevance acts as an incentive for them to focus on learning. In turn, disruptive behaviors have no chance of occurring in such classes.
• Teachers have to find ways of ensuring that students receive quick feedback on their assignments, quizzes, and tests.
• Teachers have to create systems of ensuring that students do not lose assignments. Notebooks tend to help students not lose assignments.

REFLECTION QUESTIONS

1. How are meaningful learning and classroom management related?
2. Give an example from your own experience or the experience of a colleague where skills to manage a classroom failed because of the absence of meaningful learning.

3. Why is it a teacher's responsibility to ensure that students do not lose assignments?
4. In what ways does the failure to help students turn in work in a manner that substantially reduces the risk of losing it affect a teacher?

NOTES

1. Achebe, C. (1958). *Things Fall Apart*. Portsmouth, NH: Heinemann.

Chapter Five

Managing Students' Misbehavior

*When and When Not to Respond to a Student's
Disruptive Behavior*

OBJECTIVES

1. Teachers will learn when and when not to act on some behaviors that are generally considered disruptive.
2. Teachers will learn strategies to manage challenging students.
3. Teachers will learn about other resources available in schools that they can use to manage students' behaviors.

In spite of excellent instruction and all the knowledge about how to get students to conduct themselves in nondisruptive and respectful ways, a few students may still misbehave and attempt to ruin a well-paced and purpose-driven lesson. There are a number of factors to consider in responding to a student's misbehavior.

The first and most important consideration obviously concerns the nature of the misbehavior. Is the misbehavior disrupting instruction? If it is, then it has to be dealt with promptly so that other students can continue to learn. If the answer is no, then it does not need to be addressed right away. For example, a student may be preoccupied with sending and receiving text messages. This is a form of misbehavior that interferes with the student's learning and is forbidden in most school districts.

However, notice that the student's actions, while not acceptable in a classroom, do not interfere with other students' learning. Therefore, a teacher may decide not to address such an act right away because it does not interfere with other students' learning and the teacher does not want to spend precious teaching time focusing on one student whose reaction to the teacher's remarks about using a phone in class could end up disrupting the whole learning environment.

He or she may decide to speak to the student at an appropriate time when the rest of the class is busy doing an assignment; the decision concerning whether to take action now or later needs to factor in the anticipated reaction that the teacher is going to receive from the student.

For students who are argumentative and tend to be defiant of authority, the teacher may decide it is best to address such a problem when the class's attention is not on the student; this might be at the end of the class or during a period when all the other students are occupied with some activity.

The research literature on students' misbehavior is replete with examples of students who misbehave because they seek attention. It is, therefore, not beneficial to the teacher if he or she provides such students with platforms on which the rest of the class can notice them by addressing their silly acts when the whole class is watching. To the extent possible, the teacher should attempt to minimize such students' impact on the class by finding nonattention-getting manners of discouraging them from misbehaving. For example, the teacher may just stand next to or behind such a student. Sometimes, that level of proximity to the student discourages the misbehavior.

If the misbehavior is excessive talking while the teacher is teaching, sometimes a pause by the teacher that is long enough to enable the class to realize that one or two students are talking is effective in stopping the talkers. Such measures as standing next to the student and pauses to allow the talkers to be aware of their talking should always be followed by a private discussion with the concerned students after class.

During such discussions, it is best for the teacher to be really calm and speak in a voice that does not escalate the problem. The student should be made aware that his or her excessive talking is a problem to the class and should discontinue.

It is also a very good idea at this point to send parents an e-mail or make a brief phone call to explain to them that there is a problem with the behavior of their child. For some children, the call or e-mail to parents takes care of the problem for a long time. For others, however, the call might have been expected and would be one of many calls or e-mails the teacher would have to make in the course of the school year.

WHAT TO DO WHEN A WHOLE CLASS IS TALKING

Sometimes, a class may start talking when a teacher wants to teach, and there may be several students talking at the same time. It is tempting for a teacher to feel that, in order to get the attention of the class, he or she should raise his or her voice above that of the students. Especially among new teachers, sometimes, there is the mistaken impression that students cannot hear them and, if they only raised their voices above that of the students, the students would hear them and stop talking.

Actually, students often hear perfectly what the teacher says even in the middle of their talking. So how does a teacher get several voices to stop talking and continue to teach? Frequently, a teacher is able to gain the attention of students in such a situation of general talking by deliberately lowering his or her voice as he or she begins to teach. Let the students themselves strain to hear your voice as a teacher, and soon enough you may notice that the talking dies down as students try hard to hear you.

In general, therefore, it is never a good idea to try to scream above the noise of the students. If you do the opposite, in other words, soften your voice and make it hard for those who are talking to hear you, you will find that you gain the attention of the whole class and the noise may die down on its own. If one or two students persist beyond the point where the whole class is quiet, you may want to address those students specifically by asking them to be quiet, or you may just stop talking and look at them. Often, a long pause is good enough to stop some. The truly persistent ones may need a private conversation and an e-mail or phone call to their parents.

ALWAYS BE MINDFUL OF THE WAY YOU SPEAK TO STUDENTS

While some students may talk in ways that are disrespectful, teachers should always talk and act respectfully even to such students; the best way to defuse a confrontation with a student is to talk calmly and respectfully. Displaying anger to a rude and disrespectful student exacerbates the conflict and usually ends badly for both the teacher and the student.

Whatever a teacher says to a student should never be understood by the student or the class as sarcastic or demeaning in any way; yelling is clearly counterproductive. At no point in the teacher's interactions with a student should a teacher be perceived as angry; most students, especially disruptive ones, delight in making the teacher angry.

Therefore, it does not benefit the teacher at all to look or act frustrated with a student. Often, a student who is struggling with a class's material may act out to gain the attention and respect of his or her classmates. If the teacher allows the student to ascend the platform and gain prominence in the class by being upset with his or her behavior, the student achieves his goal and will be persuaded to continue to act inappropriately from that point on.

If, on the other hand, the teacher focuses on instruction and marginalizes the student's inappropriate behavior by, perhaps, changing his or her seat quietly or telling the student calmly to stop talking and do the work on page such and such, the student may discover that he or she is unable to perturb the teacher sufficiently for him or her to lose his or her temper.

The foregoing discussion does not mean that the teacher ignores the misconduct. On the contrary, the teacher takes action. But the manner in which his or her actions are performed minimize the problem and enable the student to continue to function normally within the class.

However, after or before class, the teacher may choose to have a private conversation with the student; he or she might also decide to inform parents about the inappropriate behaviors. What is done before or after class has a greater chance of changing the student's conduct than any public showdown with the student.

Notice that the teacher does not amplify a student's misconduct by deliberately refraining from loudly and publicly addressing such misbehavior while the whole class is watching. Screaming or yelling by the teacher to a student who is misbehaving in class, in a perverse way, might be the exact response that a student is seeking from the teacher. It may be the kind of reaction sought by a student incapable of doing an assignment the teacher has set the class.

To deny such a student the high pedestal from which he or she was hoping to be viewed by the rest of the class, the teacher notes the behavior in his or her notebook and talks to the student in private at the end of class or at a time when the class is not there. If needed, the teacher further contacts the student's parents.

BUILD RELATIONSHIPS WITH STUDENTS

A really powerful tool in managing students who tend to act inappropriately is to show them that you like them. Students are particularly concerned about whether a teacher likes them or not. And those who act inappropriately, sometimes, go around thinking that the teacher dislikes them because of their behavior. In such situations, the teacher has a responsibility to build a bridge of trust with such a student.

Here is one example of where a teacher created a good relationship with a student who had started out as being very difficult.

A teacher had a student who talked excessively, laughed inappropriately, sneaked out of his seat when the teacher's back was turned, and broke pencils that he scattered on the floor. Soon, the teacher discovered that the student was extremely weak in the subject area and was at the bottom of the class in terms of his grades. However, the student gave the teacher the impression that he did not care about the class and his grades. The teacher changed his seat, which improved his behavior somewhat. But he was still a very unreliable student with regard to his behavior.

The teacher sent several e-mails to his parents and made several phone calls. He received very late responses to the e-mails, and the student's behavior did not seem to change much. The teacher decided to surround the student with students whose behaviors he could depend on; this brought about a change, and the student became less talkative because all the students around him cared about their education and did not support his efforts to disrupt.

By the end of the second quarter, with his grades at the bottom of the class, the teacher had a conference with the student's mother that went very badly, with the mother blaming the reading material, tests, quizzes, and everything she could think of for the poor performance of her child. The conference clearly showed the teacher that he could not depend on the mother to support him in improving the academic performance or behavior of her son. The student would either get moved out of his class or he would have to find a way to work with him.

In spite of the mother's anger at the teacher at the meeting and threats to move the child from the class, she did not move him out. Almost by accident, one day the child happened to be the first to arrive in the teacher's class. The teacher greeted him, "Good morning so and so." He answered back, with a smile that the teacher did not miss.

From this point on, the teacher noticed that the difficult student made a special effort to be the first to arrive, and the teacher made a point of greeting him, just as he greeted some of the first three or four students who arrived first.

The teacher also noticed that the student's behavior was improving and he seemed to volunteer to do things in the class. Each time he volunteered to do something, such as shelve books, the teacher made sure to thank him. As it dawned on the student that the teacher liked him as a person, even though he may have disapproved of his conduct at the beginning, the student became a more stable and well-mannered person in the class. By the end of the school year, it was hard for anyone in the class to associate this well-behaved student with the type of misbehavior he used to show at the beginning of the school year.

This example demonstrates the power of building relationships with some of the difficult students. While a student's misbehavior should not be condoned by a teacher, it is, however, important to avoid creating the impression that the misbehaving student is also disliked by the teacher who is exposed to such misconduct. One way of avoiding such a trap is to start afresh each day that the student comes into your class. A simple, friendly greeting at the beginning of class or a simple question that reveals a personal interest in the student may go a long way toward building a bridge of trust and confidence.

As the adults in the classrooms, teachers need to show the degree of restraint and accommodation that enable any child, regardless of how inappropriate his or her conduct was, to feel that he or she can start afresh and that the teacher does not hold grudges. After all, our interest as teachers is in what happens today and in the future in our classes. The past is relevant, but it is certainly best for us and our students that we are able to teach today and in the future and are not dragged down by a past inappropriate behavior; we need to remind ourselves that we too learned from our past mistakes when we were teenagers.

While effective teaching requires that we do not hold grudges, it does not suggest we act as if we do not know about the likely possibility of such and such a student to act inappropriately. In fact, a teacher who pretends that all students can equally be relied upon shows a level of naïveté that could be a source of serious problems for him or her in managing his or her class. The positive and negative experiences we have with our students are all critical pieces of information that we store and remember and use effectively to make decisions in our classes.

When a student acts defiantly and asks for forgiveness, we should genuinely forgive but not forget because, in the future, we may use such information to make decisions about that student. For example, in the face of requiring a student to do something in front of everyone that may be uncomfortable, we may want to eschew calling on the student who showed defiance five months ago in favor of a student who has consistently demonstrated a spirit of cooperation.

GUIDANCE COUNSELORS CAN HELP YOU

If e-mails or phone calls and endeavors to improve personal interactions with a student fail, a teacher may want to get guidance counselors involved. Usually, guidance personnel have information about children that may shed some light on their behavior. While the explanations may not excuse their behaviors, at least they give some insights into why and how to handle the concerned student. Guidance counselors may also speak to students and assist teachers in modifying their behaviors.

Sometimes, all that is needed to get a guidance counselor's assistance is a phone call or an e-mail about a student who is acting inappropriately in class. Sometimes, a guidance counselor may schedule a meeting with the student where he or she explains to the student what has been happening, or there may be a conference where all the student's teachers meet to discuss the student.

If there is a meeting involving all of the student's teachers, it is extremely important to attend such a meeting because teachers share their experiences with the student. So what seemed like aberrant behavior in one class may actually be the student's routine behavior in all classes. Hearing such information from other teachers and also learning how they deal with the student may help the teacher who is still trying to find a way to minimize the disruptive behavior of the student in his or her class.

Parents or guardians are also generally present at such conferences. This is a golden opportunity for a teacher to get to know the parents or guardians and learn how they view their child and his or her conduct in class. It is also an occasion for the teacher to explain to the parents or guardians how their child's behavior affects his or her learning and the learning of other students in the class. It is at such conferences that a teacher can obtain valuable information concerning what sort of help he or she can expect from the parents or guardians in the future. To truly be an effective teacher, one should not miss such meetings.

It is also at this type of meeting that, often, behavior intervention plans are discussed and adopted. For instance, a guidance counselor may suggest that a close monitoring of a student is needed through a daily or weekly progress report. The guidance counselor would then explain what would be involved in making such a report effective. Responsibilities of parents, teachers, the student, and the guidance counselor would be explained by the counselor. Once all have understood the way to proceed with the weekly or daily progress report, it would then begin to be implemented.

For conscientious parents who check the progress report whenever it is due to them, this method of monitoring a student's conduct and academic work can be truly beneficial to a student. A student's performance may change for the better because the parents or guardians see daily or weekly comments made by their child's teachers and take appropriate action to ensure the child's success. On the other hand, if parents do not take daily or weekly progress reports seriously, it can be a waste of time for teachers who dutifully complete them.

Fortunately, it does not take long for teachers to realize that their efforts in completing the daily or weekly progress reports are not bearing any fruit; the lack of effectiveness in the daily or weekly progress report becomes evident if the behavior of the student does not change. For instance, if nearly all the teachers comment that the concerned student is inattentive in class because of his or her phone and the behavior does not change after several progress reports have reached a parent, it becomes clear at that point that either the parent does not care to read the reports or she or he does not take the necessary actions to stop the distracting behavior. At that point, it is therefore unnecessary to continue to fill out progress reports for such a student.

USING COACHES AND CLUB SPONSORS TO MANAGE STUDENTS' BEHAVIORS

Most students are interested in sports, cheerleading, ROTC, and various clubs, such as debate, national honor society, and writers' workshop. In most school districts, students' participation in these extracurricular activities is dependent on their meeting a certain minimum GPA. Most coaches and club sponsors also require that students exhibit exemplary behavior for them to participate in their clubs and sporting organizations.

So a teacher who is aware that a certain rather disruptive or low-achieving student in his or her class also participates in a sporting activity could take advantage of the student's interest in a sporting activity to contact the coach and bring it to his or her attention.

Often, students who might not show much respect for their regular teachers have a totally different relationship with their coaches or club sponsors. The glamour, on game day, of being seen playing in, for example, a basketball or football game may be so great for a student whose parents or guardians come to watch games that students do not want to be benched because their coach is unhappy with them.

Some coaches use such leverage on players and consequently can have the kind of respect that teachers and parents may not receive from players. Thus, if a teacher contacts a coach or club sponsor about a student involved in that sport or club seeking assistance with correcting the behavior of such a student, often the results are good.

Some coaches and club sponsors realize the vital role they can play in students' lives and often require those who are interested in their sporting activities or clubs to first complete a daily or weekly progress report on their academic performance and conduct in the classes that they take. All the students' teachers fill in a form daily or weekly on the concerned students.

These kinds of forms are extremely valuable and can influence the academic and behavioral performance of students. At a minimum, the teachers filling them out become aware of the extracurricular activities of their students and also know whom to contact if an athlete's behavior or academic performance begins to cause concern for the teacher.

Ideally, all coaches and club sponsors should have a form that teachers complete for students involved in athletics or clubs. If such a uniform approach were applied to all students involved with sports and clubs, the impact on schools in terms of improved academic achievements and better behavior would be tremendous.

EXPERIENCED TEACHERS AS A RESOURCE FOR
NEW TEACHERS

Experienced teachers are one other resource for new teachers. In most schools, there are teachers who have refined their class management skills to almost a science; they just seem to know how to handle any student, and their classes are run smoothly. It is highly recommended for new teachers to take advantage of such teachers. Such teachers may become informal mentors of the new teachers and answer questions on a variety of issues affecting the new teachers.

Sometimes, new teachers may get permission from such effective teachers to occasionally get a challenging student to stay in the experienced teacher's class for a period of time so that the new teacher can get some relief. Other arrangements to help the new teacher can be made if a strong relationship has been built between the new teacher and the veteran teacher.

In some school districts, new teachers are always given mentor teachers to help them deal with the beginning of teaching, which can be extremely challenging. Mentor teachers can play an invaluable role in helping new teachers make the transition into teaching less difficult. As studies continue to show, the first three years see the greatest loses in new teachers because of the unusual challenges that teaching presents to those new to the profession.

When a school system has mentor teachers, the mentor teachers can help in providing new teachers demonstration lessons, which would show the new teacher how to present content, handle potential misbehavior, pace lessons, and many other aspects of teaching that go into effective teaching. In general, mentor teachers also provide emotional support to new teachers; new teachers do not feel alone in facing the challenges that students' misbehaviors present to them.

LEARNING WALKS AS OPPORTUNITIES FOR TEACHERS TO
LEARN FROM EACH OTHER

Learning walks is another resource for all teachers. Some schools require their teachers to take learning walks. For learning walks, teachers often meet as a team and decide to visit certain classrooms to see what and how other teachers teach. These learning walks can be very helpful to all teachers, whether one is effective or not. Learning walks allow teachers to see each other teach; these are very powerful experiences.

As teachers see each other teach and manage their classes, they get to see what others do to deal with familiar problems. Teachers are able to evaluate each other's techniques and learn lessons about what they can do in their own classrooms.

Done well, learning walks have proved to be immensely helpful to all teachers, regardless of one's years of experience in the profession.

FOCUS ON STUDENTS' STRENGTHS TO ENHANCE COOPERATION

Yet another strategy for getting students to cooperate involves accentuating their positive attributes. Some, apparently, difficult students often suffer from a sense of inadequacy in the subject area where they misbehave. Disrupting class then becomes a tool for such students to avoid the unpleasant task of learning material that they find difficult. There are several strategies for addressing such sources of disruption.

One strategy is to make the learning material accessible to even those who are severely underprepared for it. Making the material accessible does not mean diluting the content; it just means providing students the kind of supports that enable them to understand and work on difficult content. For instance, McDougal Littell's *The Language of Literature* textbook has an accompanying workbook called *The Interactive Reader*, which carries some of the readings in the main textbook but differs from the textbook because the workbook breaks down the readings into manageable chunks.

Instead of asking students to read the entire four- or five-page story and then answer questions at the very end, *The Interactive Reader* workbook breaks down the story into small segments and requires students to interact with the text by responding to a variety of prompts. Some of the prompts ask students to highlight, underline, answer basic comprehension questions, identify new vocabulary, assess, and compare and contrast. These kinds of activities help students monitor their understanding of texts that are lengthy and challenging.

Each student works at his or her own pace in the workbook. This approach ensures that, regardless of the ability level of a student, he or she benefits maximally from reading the text using *The Interactive Reader*. Each student experiences success as he or she works through the text. Where a student experiences difficulties, he or she has a chance to seek assistance immediately from the teacher or other classmates.

By reducing the level of difficulty and degree of failure, the teacher also reduces the extent to which a potential class disrupter is willing to disrupt because he or she achieves a level of success in a class where ordinarily there would always be failure.

One other way of focusing on students' strengths is by taking note of what a potentially disruptive student likes. Some students like to help shelving books, distributing supplies, cleaning the board, or being sent on errands or, generally, being helpful. If such students are not occupied with tasks like that, they may become restless and start to act in ways that could disrupt a class.

Teachers need to utilize such students by getting them to do tasks. They should also make sure that the students' helpfulness is clearly recognized with effusive words of thanks. Sometimes, all that is needed is a form of recognition for some students to behave themselves.

ADMINISTRATORS AS THE VERY LAST RESORT

The teacher's last resort in dealing with a student's inappropriate behavior is usually the school administrator or assistant principal. Generally, administrators mete out a form of punishment to a student depending on the nature of the offence. The impact of their actions tends to be rather limited; they usually do not elicit voluntary cooperation from students. Students often act in compliance out of fear instead of a genuine understanding that it is best for them to act well.

Therefore, a teacher who depends on a principal or assistant principal for managing his or her class soon finds out that the principal's or assistant principal's power to influence a permanent change in behavior is limited; he or she is better off finding solutions to his or her class's problems by himself or herself. In fact, sending a student to an administrator for class misbehavior is, in a sense, viewed by students as an acknowledgment of failure.

However, good administrators can play a constructive role in supporting teachers in the complex task of managing students' behaviors. Some can act as effective buffers between teachers and difficult parents. They can explain school policies to parents and strengthen their teachers' endeavors to teach effectively.

It is important to know, nevertheless, that the task of running a classroom falls squarely on the teacher's shoulders. Success or failure to manage a class is completely dependent on the teacher; notwithstanding their great visibility and the appearance of having a lot of power, principals and assistant principals cannot effectively substitute for a teacher in the task of managing his or her class.

KEY IDEAS IN THIS CHAPTER

- Teachers should exercise great restraint in their interactions with students. Yelling or screaming at students ultimately does not help the teacher.
- Teachers need to seek other entities within their school to help them with some challenging students. Coaches and club sponsors, for example, may help a teacher in managing the behavior of a student who is involved in extracurricular activities.

REFLECTION QUESTIONS

1. Why is it advantageous to a teacher to have students who are involved in extracurricular activities?

2. Supposing you notice that a student in your class wears an ROTC uniform once a week. He is generally well behaved but often tends to sleep during class. You have called his house phone and left messages but have not had any responses. What other alternatives do you have to correct his tendency to sleep in class?

3. How does making learning accessible to all students contribute to classroom management?

4. Why can't an assistant principal or school administrator substitute for a teacher in managing his or her class? What limitations do administrators have that impede their being effective classroom managers.

Chapter Six

Expectations of the Teacher

OBJECTIVE

Teachers will learn that, as role models to students, there are some very high expectations that come with being a teacher.

In general, teachers model for their students the behaviors that they want their students to exhibit. Because teaching involves dealing with young people, the teacher is an important role model that students have in front of them. Therefore, what the teacher says and does has great significance for the students he or she teaches; in fact, some students have trouble viewing teachers as ordinary people who go to the grocery store and live normal lives with their own children who might not be so well behaved.

For some students, teachers tend to be idealized individuals who eschew all the short-comings that "normal" people have. What are the implications of this rarefied view of teachers, and what can teachers realistically model for their students?

LANGUAGE

School districts generally discourage the use of profane or derogatory words, and most teachers insist that the language their students use in their classrooms should be free of vulgarity. Often, at the beginning of the school year, students will test a teacher's tolerance of inappropriate words by using them on each other. If a teacher appears to ignore or not respond to such usage, students conclude that such words are acceptable in his or her class. Moreover, if the teacher herself or himself uses inappropriate words, maybe in frustration, students follow the example and proceed to use such language in the class.

In short, the type of language that proliferates in a classroom reflects what the teacher has shown to the class to be acceptable. If vulgar language permeates the language of a classroom, this may be a reflection of what the teacher has permitted the students to use.

By the same token, if a class uses respectful language, it is often a demonstration of the type of language the teacher has allowed, through modeling and discouragement, to flourish in his or her class. In short, the language that is evident in a classroom is frequently a reflection of what the teacher considers acceptable.

CLEAN CLASSROOM

Similarly, the example the teacher sets with language extends to cleanliness in the classroom. Some students tend to draw or write on furniture, such as the desks they sit on. While informing a class as a whole helps in minimizing such practices, a conscientious teacher also makes sure that his or her students are not writing or drawing on their desks or other furniture in the class. The teacher can do such inspections as the students are working in the class and he or she is monitoring the class.

It can also be done daily before the first class reports to his or her class; ideally, a teacher checks the arrangement of his or her desks either at the end after the last period of the day or before the first period to ensure that the desks are where he or she wants them to be. As he or she is doing so, it is a good idea to bring along a huge eraser that can be used to erase whatever he or she sees written on the desks.

Why check the placement of desks daily? Students move desks around as lessons happen in the course of the day. To make sure that the spaces between the rows of desks are sufficient for the teacher to move around easily and to just make sure that everything is in order, it is a good idea for a teacher to daily walk around his or her class at least once, either at the end of the day or before the beginning of the first period, to straighten out the arrangement of desks. Such inspections can reveal a lot about the students who sit in those desks.

For example, a teacher may notice the student who is consistently writing things on his or her desk and decide to speak to such a student in order to get him or her to stop. The teacher may also notice that students leave their belongings behind and take them up and keep them in a secure place if there is a need to do so. For example, a student may leave a laptop behind, which the teacher may decide to keep in a locked cabinet at the end of the school day.

In other cases, a teacher may notice, at the end of the day, that a few students are leaving a lot of trash behind. He or she may decide to speak to such students so that the practice discontinues.

Furthermore, a teacher may notice that some students are not returning books to the shelf as he or she expects. Again, the teacher would obtain such information if he or she takes a tour of his or her whole class either at the end of the day after all the classes or at the beginning of the day before his or her first class; it certainly helps the teacher to do this on a daily basis.

PUNCTUALITY AND ATTENDANCE

Punctuality is another area where a teacher's behavior has an influence on students. If a teacher routinely comes to class on time and requires of his or her students to do the same, the majority of the students will follow the example and come to class on time; please realize that there will always be one or two in any class who will struggle with punctuality or any class requirement for that matter.

In teaching, the teacher's success at any endeavor is not going to be measured by reaching 100 percent compliance or participation because students are individuals with their own differences. If 96 percent of the students regularly report to class on time, this should be considered a high rate of success, even if three or four students just cannot come to class on time.

Observe, however, that if the teacher is routinely late, it becomes difficult to insist that students come on time. In fact, when the teacher is frequently late, it is impossible to take note of students who are late. If the teacher comes to class on time one day in the week and decides to take action on students who arrived late, students are quick to notice the hypocrisy and might not react favorably to an infraction that the teacher is guilty of himself or herself.

Additionally, teachers who are usually late create a great deal of inconvenience to other teachers who have classrooms near them. When a teacher is late, for example, his or her students may not enter the classroom when the bell has gone for doing so. As a result, they may become a source of disruption or noise to other classrooms near them. The uncertainty about when such a teacher will appear creates problems for the person in charge of substitute teachers. She or he may be uncertain whether or not to assign a substitute teacher to the class whose regular teacher is late.

Sometimes, other teachers who might be in his or her planning period are asked to cover the class until the teacher appears. Such teachers may feel imposed upon. In any case, students lose instructional time because of the regular teacher's lateness; if this happens often, the teacher's standing among students and colleagues drops substantially because of being perceived as unreliable. Therefore, it is advisable for a teacher to set a good example to students on punctuality by coming to class on time regularly.

Attendance is another area where a teacher's example is vital. Effective teachers are rarely absent, and when they are absent, it is for a good reason. A teacher's regular attendance has a tremendous impact on his or her students' learning. Teachers, students, and parents know that, when a teacher is absent and a substitute teacher runs a class, often, not much gets done.

Generally, substitute teachers are not expected to teach. As a result, they are usually assigned classes not on the basis of their subject expertise; in fact, it is routinely common to find a substitute teacher assigned a class about which he or she has no knowledge at all.

For example, a substitute teacher who does not speak French may find himself or herself "teaching" a French class. In most cases, a substitute teacher's role is really one of ensuring that students behave themselves reasonably well in the absence of the regular teacher. Good substitute teachers are, therefore, those who have superior skills in maintaining discipline in the classes they are assigned.

If the substitute teacher's role is one of maintaining order in the classroom and not of teaching, it thus follows that, whenever a teacher is absent, his or her students lose on instruction. If a teacher, for example, is absent for a month during a school year, his or her students have lost one month of learning, which is twenty days of schooling. If the school has a hundred teachers and each teacher is absent twenty days in a year, the total number of lost school days in a year for the students is a staggering two thousand days.

While this is an extreme example because most teachers accumulate ten or fewer absences per school year, the example still points to the serious impact that teachers' absences have on students' learning. It follows then that a teacher's absence needs to be for a valid reason.

Teachers who take a day off to celebrate their birthdays or to just enjoy a spring day need also to realize the impact their actions have on the learning of their students. Teachers who are serious about improving their students' learning agonize over taking a day off; such teachers will take a leave day for their illness or the illness of their children or spouses.

Besides directly affecting students' learning, a teacher's frequent absences demoralize both parents and students. Soon after parents and students learn that such and such a teacher takes numerous absences, they grumble and feel powerless and, sometimes, resentful for a behavior they have no control over.

Often, such absences also affect the climate in the classroom because of lack of consistency in classroom management. The numerous substitute teachers who cover the class bring a lot of instability to the class; this can result in a class becoming hard to manage, even if the regular teacher has excellent classroom management skills. In short, teachers should not allow themselves to take frivolous absences because their absences do directly affect students' learning.

APPEARANCE

While there is no appearance code for teachers, there is an understanding among experienced teachers that they have to present themselves in an exemplary manner. This involves both grooming and dress. In some school districts, students are not allowed to wear certain clothes. For example, clothes that promote drugs or gang activity or that show a lot of bare skin may not be permitted to be worn on school grounds. Teachers are required to enforce such dress rules.

At the same time, though, it is expected that teachers themselves would not wear such clothes. So, while there is no dress code for teachers, it would seem hypocritical for teachers to exempt themselves from following a dress code that they insist their students follow.

What female students are not allowed to wear has often been an area of contention. In some school districts, female students are not allowed to wear very short dresses or skirts; they are also not allowed to wear see-through clothes or clothes that reveal a lot of their uncovered bodies. Other districts discourage female students from wearing blouses or tops that are bare in the back or expose the stomach.

While female teachers are not told that they are bound by the same regulations that apply to the female students, it is implied that what is not good for the students may also not be good for teachers. In other words, female teachers seem hypocritical if they require their students not to wear clothes that reveal a lot of their bodies while they themselves wear such clothes. Because teachers are role models for their students, they too have to be exemplary in the way that they dress.

THE IMPORTANCE OF KEEPING RECORDS

There are three primary people affecting a teacher's professional life: students, parents, and administrators. When things are going well, parents and administrators are largely invisible to the teacher. Thus, the teacher may get the illusion that students are the only people whom he or she works for. However, whenever a problem arises, it becomes quickly obvious that parents or guardians have always been lurking in the shadows of each student.

It is, therefore, very important for a teacher to always factor in parents or guardians and administrators as he or she is going about his or her professional work. How does one always ensure that one would be able to provide required documentation whenever it is needed?

Evidence is critical for whatever conclusions or decisions a teacher makes. For example, if a teacher sends an e-mail or makes a call to a parent concerning a student, he or she has to create a system for keeping a record of such an event. A simple notebook can work to record the name of the student about whom a call was made, date and time of the call, phone number, reason for the call, and whom the teacher spoke to.

Recording such information on sticky notes or scraps of paper is ineffective because those bits and pieces of paper are likely to be lost and the record for the parental contact would be lost too.

With e-mail, the easiest way to keep a record of an e-mail sent to a parent or guardian is to send oneself a copy of the e-mail. In that way, the teacher has a record of the interaction he or she had with a parent or guardian.

In situations where a teacher's decision is being challenged by a parent or guardian concerning a student, such records can provide evidence of what the teacher has done before arriving at a certain decision. For example, a teacher may decide to change the seat of a certain student because of that student's excessive talking. The student may not want the seat change, perhaps arguing that she or he works well in the seat that she or he currently occupies.

If this simple matter escalates to involve a parent or guardian who might want to support his or her child, the teacher may point to several phone calls or e-mails that he or she has made concerning the student's excessive talking and why, at this point in time, he or she has concluded that it is best to change the student's seat.

When such a case is being made, it always helps if a teacher can mention specific dates when a phone call was made or an e-mail was sent to report the behavior; instead of vague recalls about a contact made in the past, the degree of specificity impresses upon the parent or guardian about the teacher's serious approach to the matter at hand. As a result, it may lead to a quick resolution of the problem.

Other kinds of records are more vital than the ones indicated above. Students' attendance records, for example, play an extremely important role in revealing the kind of student one is. On the basis of attendance alone, one can show a strong correlation with academic performance. In other words, students who regularly attend school tend to do well. Inversely, students who are frequently absent tend to not do well. Carefully kept attendance records can help a teacher make a case for why a student is not doing well in his or her class.

If a student misses a class or two each week and the records are well maintained and reveal such absences, a parent who might want to argue that she or he does not understand why his or her child is failing would be referred to such a record to see a connection between the child's attendance and his or her grade in the class.

It is important to observe that, while keeping good records is vital, it is equally important that the teacher takes time to inform parents or guardians about those records, especially when the record shows that the student is being adversely affected. In the case of a student who is frequently absent, a teacher has the primary responsibility to contact parents or guardians concerning those absences so that a change in behavior can occur. Because frequent absences are often noncontroversial, a teacher could easily communicate such information through a brief e-mail.

Other attendance matters require instant action. For instance, there are cases when a student decides to miss one class but attends others where a call to a parent may have to be made immediately. Cutting class, in the usual parlance, is the type of behavior that can be stopped quickly if a teacher takes immediate action.

Usually, when students learn from their classmates that such and such a teacher calls parents as soon as he or she suspects that a student has missed his or her class without a good reason, most of them may not dare to cut that class in the future.

For students with IEPs or 504 plans, good record keeping plays a critical role as well. A teacher has to be aware of the specific details of a particular student's accommodations. Most accommodations deal with allowing a student extended time for assignments and tests. A teacher needs to be aware of such information and should make sure that the concerned student is afforded extended time when he or she asks for it.

Other common accommodations tend to do with seating arrangements. Usually, a student who is ADD or ADHD may need to sit in front of the class or in an area with the least distractions. These kinds of accommodation are easy to make and should be made.

ONE-ON-ONE INTERACTIONS BETWEEN TEACHERS AND STUDENTS

When a teacher meets with a student in his or her classroom during planning, at lunch, or after school, there are several precautions that he or she has to take to make sure that such a meeting is perceived as safe for the student. If possible, the student can come with a buddy who is not part of the meeting and might sit at a distance from where the meeting is taking place.

Alternatively, the teacher can make sure that the door to his or her classroom is wide open so that people passing by can see into the classroom as the meeting with the student is taking place; it is also advisable to leave windows uncovered so that people passing by the classroom can see into the room.

If the meeting is happening after school, a teacher may tell a student to meet in an area where there are other students. For example, a meeting could be held in the library if the library tends to have other students after school. It could also be held in a corner in the gymnasium or cafeteria or in a hallway where other students are around.

Generally, it is not a good idea to have a one-on-one meeting with a student in one's classroom with the door closed, windows covered, or after school when the school is almost empty of other students. Such meetings have a high potential of being misconstrued and can lead to unfortunate repercussions for teachers involved. If a teacher has to meet a student alone, let the meeting be in an area where other students or teachers can see the two meeting.

If a teacher is meeting a student on account of a dispute or some disagreement he or she has had with that student, it is even more necessary that such a meeting should occur in an open space where other students or teachers can see the two, even though they may not hear what they are talking about. Most students are honest and really good people; however, there have been cases reported in recent years of students who have lied to their parents and school authorities on teachers' supposed inappropriate behavior that has ended up putting such teachers in trouble.

On the other hand, there have also been a plethora of stories of teachers acting inappropriately with students, and such stories have been shown to be true. Therefore, to ensure that students feel safe, it is necessary when a teacher meets a student one-on-one that it is done in an area where the student feels and is seen to be safe. Under such conditions, the teacher also feels secure in the knowledge that the encounter with the student is being witnessed by other students and teachers.

WHAT IS AN ASSAULT?

Related to meeting students one-on-one is also the issue of what a student may perceive as an assault. Many teachers would be shocked to learn that, technically, an assault can be construed to have occurred at any point when a teacher touches a student, regardless of the physical impact of the touch. Even a light touch of the finger on a student's body can be said to be a form of assault on that student. An assault occurs whenever the receiver of the touching perceives it as such.

What does this mean for a teacher? It means that teachers, especially in middle and high schools, should refrain from touching students. Sounds cold! When a teacher is angry or unhappy with a student's behavior, it is critical that he or she should particularly refrain from touching a student because such a touch could likely be perceived as a physical assault by the student. When a teacher looks unhappy or is angry with a student, the student may feel physically threatened by this adult who looks large and threatening.

If the teacher goes further to touch the student on the shoulder as he or she is asking the student to do something, such as leave the classroom, the student may interpret the touching as a form of shoving because the teacher is huge and angry. Thus, the student may report that light touch on the shoulder by the teacher as a forceful shoving. It is therefore especially advisable not to touch students when a teacher or a student is angry.

KEY IDEAS IN THIS CHAPTER

- Teachers are role models for students and as such should exhibit exemplary behavior.
- Even though there are no rules for how teachers have to dress, if there are dress codes for students, teachers should show by example that they too comply with those dress codes.
- Teachers need to develop good record-keeping systems because, from time to time, teachers have to demonstrate to parents or administrators why certain decisions were made.
- Meetings with individual students should be done in areas where other adults and students are around, even though they may not hear what is being discussed.

REFLECTION QUESTIONS

1. Why is it particularly necessary for a teacher to meet an angry student or one with whom the teacher has had a difference of opinion in an open space where other students and teachers are present?
2. If an assault is critically dependent on the perspective of the receiver of the assault, what troubling questions does this raise for teachers in general?
3. What can school districts do to protect teachers from frivolous claims of assaults by immature and vindictive students?

Epilogue

Effective classroom management as presented in this book is intertwined with high academic achievement for students. In addition, effective classroom management is, in essence, quite different from discipline. Discipline is reactive to situations of misbehavior and tends to impose punishments, whereas effective classroom management is integral to teaching and preempts rather than reacts to occurrences of misconduct.

Ideally, a teacher recognizes and nips in the bud nascent behaviors that, if not attended to, would blossom into acts of disruptive conduct. The managing of such potentially disruptive conduct is not a separate component of teaching, but is concurrent with teaching and learning. At its best, effective classroom management is nonintrusive in the lesson and occurs while the majority of the students are gainfully engaged in learning; in other words, the students who are the subject of the teacher's attention are not given any prominence in the class by the teacher stopping everything to address their off-task behavior. Instead, the teacher unobtrusively attends to them as the learning continues uninterrupted.

This notion of effective classroom management, which is inseparable from effective teaching and continual monitoring of students' behavior, assumes a high level of preparation and involvement on the part of the teacher. First, the basic furniture aspects of the classroom have to be in place before students enter the classroom on that first day of the school year. For example, syllabi, seating charts, classroom decorations, rules, procedures, websites for homework, and other class information all have to be ready before students enter one's classroom on the first day of the school year.

Second, the teacher needs to be alert to the brief critical window of opportunity that opens during the first two weeks of the school year to establish procedures and expectations for his or her class. Teachers need to fully utilize the two-week period of relative peace to establish firmly their expectations for students' learning and class conduct.

Every teacher needs to honestly ask himself or herself at the beginning of the school year how he or she wants the class to look like for the rest of the year. Should students read quietly when he or she wants them to? Should students be quiet when they are taking tests and quizzes? Should students wait for the teacher's signal when the bell goes for dismissal at the end of class? Should, students get permission to obtain tissues, or can they just get up and do so without permission? What other things are important to the teacher?

All these important points need to be thought out carefully by the teacher, and those that he or she considers important should be codified into class rules. Class rules present a summary of what the teacher considers critical guidelines for how students will behave in his or her class for the rest of the school year. Most teachers want respect from students and include such a rule in the class rules. It is best to phrase class rules in such a general way that they capture most instances in which the rule may be manifested.

Also important to managing classes well are the teacher's goals for his or her classes. Identifying yearlong goals for one's classes provides all yearlong purpose and critical focus for one's efforts. The sense of a sustained momentum and urgency that prevails in well-managed classes often stems from the teacher's awareness about what he or she wants the class to achieve by the end of the school year or semester.

A goal such as improving students' writing requires many things to be achieved. In addition to writing itself, such a goal would require students' reading to improve. Improvement in reading leads to expansion in vocabulary, improvements in sentence construction deriving from the models of good writing the students are exposed to. In short, it is relatively easy to sustain focus on instruction if the teacher has set goals for his or her classes. The goals provide a rationale for what happens in the classroom every day. Therefore, every lesson is indeed a small step in the yearlong journey of achieving the goals that the teacher has set for his or her class.

Thus, classroom management and effective teaching are intricately intertwined, even though certain aspects of classroom management, such as class preparations before school starts, necessarily precede actual teaching. However, once both are in place, a well-managed class simultaneously displays effective classroom management and effective teaching.

SELECTED REFERENCES

Achebe, C. (1958). *Things Fall Apart.* Portsmouth, NH: Heinemann.
Evertson, C. M., & Weinstein, C. S. (Eds.). (2006). *Handbook of classroom management: Research, practice, and contemporary issues.* Mahwah, NJ: Lawrence Erlbaum Publishers.

Wong, H., & Wong, R. (1991). *The first days of school: How to be an effective teacher.* Mountain View, CA: Harry K. Wong Publications.

About the Author

Andrew T. Kulemeka, PhD, obtained his Bachelor of Education with Distinction degree at the University of Malawi, Master of Arts at the Australian National University, and Doctor of Philosophy in linguistics at Indiana University, Bloomington. He taught at universities in the United States and Malawi before spending twenty years teaching English in Prince George's County Public Schools. Most of those years were spent mentoring new and struggling teachers at Bowie High School, where he earned a reputation for being the best and most demanding teacher in the English Department.

He was formally certified as a mentor teacher and also trained as a principal. Thus, he understands teaching from three professional perspectives: as a teacher, a mentor teacher, and an administrator. It is these three points of view and his twenty years of teaching grade school children that he brings to bear in his analysis of what strategies work in managing classrooms.

Kulemeka has also published a grammar of Chichewa, his native language, which is spoken in Malawi, Mozambique, and Zambia. He also coauthored with Robert Botne a bilingual dictionary of Chichewa and English, which was published in Germany. He is also a published author of short stories, some of which are currently being studied in high schools in Malawi.